CITY
WITCHERY

Brimming with creative inspiration, how-to projects, and useful
information to enrich your everyday life, Quarto Knows is a favorite
destination for those pursuing their interests and passions. Visit our
site and dig deeper with our books into your area of interest:
Quarto Creates, Quarto Cooks, Quarto Homes, Quarto Lives,
Quarto Drives, Quarto Explores, Quarto Gifts, or Quarto Kids.

Author: Lisa Marie Basile
Illustration: Victoria Nelson: pages 13, 17, 27, 28, 30, 34, 35, 73, 74, 80, 83, 84, 89, 94, 98, 117,
127, 129, 135; all others: Shutterstock.com

Printed in 06/21, Singapore.

MIX
Paper from
responsible sources
FSC™ C007207

#334743

CITY
WITCHERY

LISA MARIE BASILE

becker&mayer! books

DEDICATION

For all the poets, dreamers, changemakers, and witches who believe in the power of places and portals. And for all the people (and guardian angels) who sent me safely on my own wild journeys through space and place.

TABLE OF CONTENTS

"You take delight not in a city's seven or seventy wonders, but in the answer it gives to a question of yours."

—ITALO CALVINO, *Invisible Cities*

BEGIN

AN INTRODUCTION
TO THIS BOOK, CITY WITCHERY,
AND MY KIND OF MAGIC

F MAKING MAGIC IS A TOOL for influencing events, creating from intention, and alchemizing ideas into realities, then a city is surely a witch's muse.
Think of all the ideas and art and movements—and magic!—born of cities big
and small.

In my city, New York City, witches are everywhere. They're marching for
LGBTQIA rights. They're covering the bridges in flowers to support Black
lives. They're engaging in feverish conversations about dreams in crowded
sidewalk bars. They're pulling tarot cards on picnic blankets, on buses, in cafes.
These acts of splendid humanity are sacred to me—to all of us. Because cities
are places where we enchant and conjure, build community, and make change.
That's the energy of the city witch.

You're probably one of us.

In this book, we're going to explore the magic of dazzling, tiring, flawed, and
beautiful cities (and city living, like making magic in an apartment). We're going
to get to know our city's noises and shapes and shadows and languages and
changes and ghosts—and we are going to self-explore, self-care, intuit, create,
write, travel, and make magic in it. We are going to play in the light and shadow
from our bedrooms and fire escapes, beneath skyscrapers, and on public
transportation.

And we're going to dispel the idea that only nature can make a witch. You don't *need* a dewy green meadow or a backyard garden or a beach property to experience magic. You don't *need* pure silence or a sky full of stars. You don't *need* expensive tools. You just need your intention, an open mind, and some creativity.

THE INSPIRATION BEHIND THIS BOOK

This book came to me during the COVID-19 crisis in New York City—which is ongoing as I write this—when our city made global headlines for being a hotspot. It was the hardest year for me; I'm sure this is true for you. I hope by the time this book is in your hands, your city will be healing.

I have been in mourning, watching my city build makeshift hospitals in anchored ships and in the convention center where I graduated. I spent much of this time reflecting on the changing energies of my city, experiencing the gloom of silence and the awe of public ritual.

For months, each night at 7:00 p.m., my fellow city dwellers pulled out pots and pans and sent their clamoring sounds into the skies and streets below as a way of thanking the essential workers caring for the sick and the dearly departed. I knew cities around the country and world were doing this too—this collective ritual that served as a message, a bonding, and a way of summoning and directing energy to the people who needed it most. It was a ritual of unity. And when I clanked my pots together on rooftops, it was city magic.

Confined in my apartment, it became clear my relationship to my city had changed now that I had less access to it—and the few masked solo walks I could take would have to be made extra magical. So I found hidden corners to meditate and peopleless spots at the Seaport to work with water energies. And even though it was always lovely to have space to think and *just be*, I found the missing energy of the city meant more to me than I'd realized.

I have had many powerful magical experiences in New York: Leading a grief-and-death poetic ritual in Brooklyn's Green-Wood Cemetery—where hundreds of people got comfortable with the thinning of the veils. Volunteering at a soup kitchen. Taking to my New York City rooftop to eat ancestral foods and make a summer altar with friends. Spending hours at the Metropolitan Museum of Art, soaking in the history and being creatively inspired by the energies around me. Riding a subway and drawing symbols of protection into my palm when the car broke down in a dark tunnel underground. Creating self-care rituals after commuting back and forth from New York City to New Jersey everyday for two years (and creating energy protective shields while walking through Port Authority). Realizing my wallet had been stolen and having a stranger give me money and a Metrocard with which to get to work. This was *my* city magic—and this book is inspired by all of it.

What is your city magic, or what kind of city magic do you hope for?

THE MAGIC OF THE CITYSCAPE IS IN MY BLOOD

I've got city energy deep in my blood. Born in a small city in the New York metropolitan area, I have been living in the city for about two decades. Today, I live a block from the World Trade Center and City Hall, two spaces of immense energy. In these spaces, I've watched humanity grieve and grow, protest and resist.

New York City (I've lived in nearly every borough!) has shaped who I've become—writing poems and casting spells on rooftops and stoops, visiting botanicas and bodegas to buy candles and smoke-cleansing supplies, keeping my altars or sacred spaces collapsible or undetectable so my roommates wouldn't notice, and visiting community gardens and cemeteries during long, meditative walks.

The great energy of city life lives within me. My Sicilian grandparents—who emigrated from cities themselves (Naples and Palermo)—landed here in New York City, making homes for themselves in Brooklyn and New Jersey. I imagine my ancestors shopping for fresh herbs in clamoring piazzas under the hot sun, hanging colorful linens and undergarments from apartment building clotheslines, and contending with fascist officers out in the streets.

My other set of great-grandparents left Russia and Poland to descend on a new life in cities in New Jersey. It was a struggle for my family—financially, culturally, and in other ways I can't imagine. And it was a struggle for me.

As a teenager, I was in foster care in New Jersey; once I aged out and came to New York City, I was thrown into a wild world of change and movement and opportunity, working endless hours to survive on very little money. It had (and has) its ups and downs and its beauties and deep problems but I used the lessons I learned to create a sacred life for myself, to help myself and others. I think, in some ways, the city helped me find myself after trauma—and build myself into who I'd become.

Of course, all of this isn't to say the inherent magic of a rural or sleepy coastal town doesn't make me swoon. I don't need cement and skyscrapers to feel the power. My father lives in Kentucky; he has a massive green backyard (where his pet pig lives), and when we drink coffee in the morning, we are surrounded by plants and bees and birdsong. My grandmother Dorothy was raised in the mountains of Virginia under a cover of stars. When visiting my brother in New Orleans, I'd walk through the French Quarter to feel its intense, rich magic and history.

I have nothing but love for nature and those kinds of magic—but for now, I live in the city (and find myself traveling to cities here and abroad—Glasgow, London, Los Angeles—fairly often for family purposes). So here we are, city witching.

WHAT YOU CAN EXPECT FROM THIS BOOK

This book is for *anyone* who wants to develop a sacred practice, explore the inner self, and tap into everyday, walking-down-the-street magic while living in a city or traveling through one. You don't have to be a witch or align yourself with the witch archetype (although you probably do if you are reading this!), nor do you have to practice or believe anything. It's about discovering *your own magic* within the context of a city environment.

This book is my offering, and my take, on ritual and sacredness within a city. It is inspired by my life in New York City, my own eclectic magical practice, my background in creative writing, trauma healing, and my focus on accessibility.

City Witchery takes pages out of my previous two books, *Light Magic for Dark Times* and *The Magical Writing Grimoire*—both of which embrace an adaptable, trauma-informed, intuitive, shadow-work-rich, writing-based magic. This magic is a collaboration between you, your city, and the prompts in this book.

You will be gently and safely guided, but you can always make it your own. It is full of prompts, meditations, and reflections—and a bit of my own story.

I invite you to wander, write, and engage in accessible ritual with me—and with the city. In these pages, you will:

· Discover *your own magic* within the context of a city environment.
· Travel with intention to other cities
· Embrace the enchantment of city streets and the power of wandering
· Write poetry and tell stories of place
· Find ways to make your apartment accessible and sacred
· Reframe city limitations and find potential and inspiration
· Create daily rituals that ground and soothe amid chaos
· Self-protect and self-care when oversaturated and overwhelmed
· Envision magical ways to give back to your community

WHAT *SHOULDN'T* YOU EXPECT FROM THIS BOOK?

City Witchery isn't meant to be an introductory or explanatory book on witchcraft—at all. It doesn't claim to be the Definitive Practice of City Magic; it's not the first book on the topic and it won't be the last. It's not a thorough grimoire of spells; it's not based on any specific practice or path (although you're encouraged to pull in any gods or deities from your own practice!). I work mostly with energy, archetypes, and intention.

I encourage you to research *numina* or *genius loci* (meaning a guardian deity or presiding spirits of a place). A great book that delves more into that is *Urban Magick: A Guide for the City Witch* by Diana Rajchel.

If you associate a certain city with an archetype, god, or deity, please feel free to work with them and invite them into your space! For example, the Statue of Liberty may be considered a spirit in New York City. Inhabited by divinity or not, she is a symbol of freedom, love, compassion, and inclusion—and that is magical.

SO, WHO *IS* THIS BOOK FOR?

This book is for city dwellers, wanderlusters, travelers, poets, dreamers, witches, rebels, community builders, and creators. It's for people who eschew labels. It's for both the quiet types who prefer to cast spells at their bedroom altars and the bold types who love to get out into the busy streets to feel the energy.

I invite you to use this book in any way that speaks to *you*. Adapt it to your own practice and beliefs. Collapse my prompts into your own ritual experiences. You are encouraged to adapt parts of rituals, turn a walking meditation into a still one, or to write your own incantations (which I *always* recommend!).

Take what works, leave what doesn't, and expand it into something you can call your own.

REFRAMING CITY MAGIC, ACCESSIBILITY, AND ADAPTABILITY

As a magic-making word witch, chronic illness patient, and disability advocate, I focus deeply on what is accessible. I've had to. I live in a huge city that makes things challenging—whether that's in having enough money, climbing up and down stairs on a flare-up day, or finding a scrap of uninhabited space upon which to pray or meditate or think.

And so, as this book says, *Let's get flexible. You are already magical enough.* You can be a magical being in your apartment, on the subway, or in your local park—no arcane knowledge or permission needed.

But what about the lack of nature? I've had to adapt my practice and make it meaningful to me outside of having easy, quick access to nature (although there's always more nature than you may think) and that's okay. We'll explore not only developing our relationship with nature but also learning to find and tune into what we *do have.*

And what about small spaces? Yep. Cities are all about the cramped apartment life—but you *can* make it work. Usually, my altars are stored in boxes or bags, or splayed out upon smallish windowsills; when I open the window, New York City's music pours in, washing over my plants, stones, photographs, or scrolls of paper. That Big Energy feels like home to me because I choose to feel its creativity, its hope, and its goodness that exists in many people who do exist here. Where people in rural areas may have their own herb gardens and access to— sigh, dreamy!—direct moonlight, us city folk have all that oh-so-intense *energy.*

And the chaos and unpredictability and tiresomeness of it all? I say, let's use it. Let's wander. Let's learn. Let's find enchantment in the unpredictable. Let's look past the noises and messiness and see a resilient community. Let's apply self-care to our city lives; let's focus on what is good and try to preserve it through outreach and awareness. Let's take care of ourselves (and others) within the city. Let's shadow work and explore limitations. And let's create beauty and poetry along the way.

I truly hadn't realized how important the city experience was to me until it challenged me to not only reframe what is sacred (since it is so often looped together with nature and quiet and Instagrammable #Cottagecore aesthetics), but also asked me to find peace and inspiration in adaptability.

I think a huge part of the city experience is the feeling of "what's next?"—on a personal and global level—and this book contemplates that question. Living in a city pressed me to question myself, to look deeper, to ask myself what I truly want.

A NOTE ON ACCESSIBILITY

In these pages, you will see sections on wandering and rituals that include walking meditations. If you are not ambulatory or aren't ambulatory sometimes, there are various ways to tap into all the magic mentioned here. First, you can adapt *anything*—or skip to the sections that *do* speak to you. I have tried to include practices that are for both indoors and outdoors in city spaces. I also deeply recommend you call occult shops, museums, event spaces, or spaces you wish to visit ahead of time to see if they are accommodating to wheelchairs or offer seating arrangements for folks who can't stand or sit for long periods. Those who are sensitive to lights and sounds should prepare likewise.

One idea that came from my ankylosing spondylitis community: YouTube offers a deluge of people's videos of city visits that you can watch to get a sense of energy and inspiration. Many are GoPro point-of-view videos that take you on a trip. I've watched many of these before visiting cities to get a sense of the energy. I encourage you to watch travel series and documentaries too. If you can get out and into a cafe or a park here and there, that will be a good time to pull out your journal. Simply opening your window and feeling the energy can be helpful as well. Please adapt as necessary.

I'm not sure I would have crafted such an eclectic, introspective, ever-changing personal practice had I not been forced to think, *What works for me? What do I have on hand? How can I find magic in my home—in my body—surrounded by the clamoring of bodies and energies and oh-so-much cement? How can I get creative and inspired?*

SACRED TOOLS AND AIDS, OR WHAT YOU'LL NEED TO WORK WITH THIS BOOK

I aim to keep the supplies list extremely bare, as intention and energy are at the core of this book and accessibility is important to me. Please feel free to swap or update as needed.

As Laura Tempest Zakroff writes so eloquently in *Weave the Liminal*, "Tools are designed to assist us. The ability to use them comes from within us, not them. A wand can help you direct energy, but it is not where the power resides."

- **A city grimoire, otherwise known as a journal.** Your "city grimoire" is going to be the most important tool here (you can literally leave everything else if necessary). Because this book is all about self-exploration, you'll find many prompts are for reflection. You're going to want a journal that is substantial— something that you dedicate to the experiences within this book.

  Make sure it's something you don't mind carrying around in your bag or on your person as you move through the city. For those of you who don't write (Hi, I have arthritic hands!), please feel free to use a voice recorder or anything else that works for *you*. You may want to capture city images and sounds too.

- **Candles.** There are some rituals throughout the book that ask you to use a candle. I keep a bag of tea lights for easy ritual purposes. If you can't burn a candle in your space, simply find an object to focus on.

- **Kitchen supplies.** While not necessary by any means, we will be discussing kitchen witchery—making food with intention—so if you have solitary access to a kitchen (hard when you have roomies, I know) for ritual purposes here and there, that would be good.

- **Altar items that bring you joy, inspire you, ground you, and empower you.** This may include statues, symbols, tarot cards, candles, shells, rocks, crystals, gifts, knickknacks, pentagrams, tea towels, jewelry, perfume, images of saints or rosaries, prayer beads, anointing oils, sigils, fabrics, books, photographs, handmade items, etc. These are ALL up to you.

- **An altar space.** This may be a windowsill, a shelf with some space, a bedside table, or even a moveable altar (such as a bag or box or bedside table where you keep your magical items). I use one single shelf in my bedroom and a part of my windowsill in my living room.

- **Items that represent cities and your place within them.** This may include items you found while wandering your city or traveling to other cities. Think creatively here; you can use a bus ticket, a MetroCard, a well-used map, keys, a touristy knickknack, that beautiful dress you bought in Madrid, or a photograph of yourself in the city.

- **Access to one windowsill, a stoop, a back garden, or a roof.** This is for moon water purposes.

- **Space cleansing and clearing supplies (optional).** You can do a smoke cleanse by burning sprigs of lemon balm, rosemary, pine, or cedar (sage is deeply over-harvested, so try to buy ethically harvested sage if you do use it) or find an herb your ancestors would have used (my Mediterranean ancestors would have used rosemary or olive leaves). Of course, be cautious of roommates, allergies, pets, and very sensitive smoke detectors. Because of small apartments and smoke detectors, you can instead make a spray bottle with some lemon, water, and essential oil to spritz before doing a cleansing of your space. Lastly, some people are sensitive to scents! Totally okay. In this case, skip herbs and use pure moon water (see **Moon Water Magic pp. 86**).

- **Crystals (optional).** I use crystals as symbols of certain energies and feelings (see **Crystals for City Witches pp. 78**). I may recommend a few crystals throughout the book, but they're optional. If you want to work with them, I recommend carrying them through your city experiences, using them on your altar, and meditating on the energy you feel when holding them.

WHAT IS A CITY, EXACTLY?

There are *many* fascinating city archetypes and definitions (and they definitely differ from country to country). Often, it comes down to size and population density, continuous inhabitation ("city" derives from "civitas," which is Latin for civilization), and the greater role a place plays and the influence it has (the Greeks say "metropolis," or "mother city").

No matter what kind of city *you* live in or travel to—coastal, sky-scraper-adorned, expansive and densely populated, smaller but tourist-drenched—you are a city witch.

Each city is its own living, breathing mosaic (or mosaics)—changed by its many people, the powers that be, gentrification and finances, general culture, subcultures, communities of artists and thinkers, the landscape, the history, and the energies or archetypes that inhabit it and give it its robust and complex identity(ies).

In ancient China, people embraced feng shui—a practice of arranging things according to energy flow—in their city planning. Cities were designed with landscape, mythology, and astrology in mind to create balance between the energy of the people and the land.

A city invariably affects who we are, our wellness, and how we expand and grow as individuals and as a society. You and I may not be able to plan our cities, but city magic gets us to think about those ancient concepts: harmony, balance, and good energy. Once we start noticing where things are, how buildings and statues make us feel, and our proximity to nature and certain neighborhoods, we can get a feel for that same energy flow.

A NOTE ON CITY LIFE & MENTAL HEALTH

City life—for a host of reasons—has been associated with mental health struggles, particularly with anxiety and depression, according to Kevin Bennett, PhD, a teaching professor in social-personality psychology and fellow at the Centre for Urban Design and Mental Health in London.

Some mental health issues disproportionately affect marginalized groups—and they're associated with all sorts of issues, from job loss and homelessness to serious social isolation. For this reason, it's important to note that while *City Witchery* provides a guide to tending to your sense of sacredness within a city, it is no substitute for mental health care. You are loved and deserve care if you are struggling.

ILLUMINATE

TAPPING INTO
AND USING ENERGIES

GROUNDING, CLEANSING, ENERGY WORK
AND JOURNALING

When preparing for journaling, engaging in ritual, or sloughing off the energetic residue of the outside world (or shielding oneself from it), a few important techniques will help.

Below, we'll explore grounding energy, raising energy, shielding ourselves from energies, and cleansing ahead of ritual.

DROPPING ANCHOR:
GROUNDING IN THE HERE AND NOW

Having a solid, go-to grounding exercise is key in any sort of magical or sacred practice. Finding grounding allows us to soothe our nervous system (which is *especially* important in a busy, chaotic city; I've had a few too many panic attacks in crowded, rush-hour subway cars) and it readies our bodies to receive, transmit, and feel energy. Grounding helps us tune into an anchor point, rid ourselves of excess energies, and find balance. The following are a few easy ways to ground:

• **Breath work**. Breath in for five seconds, hold for five seconds, breath out for five seconds. Imagine the inhalation as luminous and shimmering if this helps. Imagine the exhalation as the breath of tension, excess energy, and pent-up "muck" from other beings, circumstances, and places you've been. This is great when you've navigated a dodge-out-of-the-way transit hub or if you've been stuck in bumper-to-bumper traffic while watching the seconds tick away. It's also great if you've visited a site where a tragedy took place and you find yourself needing to come back to yourself after experiencing heightened emotions.

- **Earthing.** Put your bare feet onto the earth—in a local park or in a strip of back garden. Water works too. Quietly envision your excess energy draining into the earth below, being collected, absorbed, and neutralized. Studies show earthing can calm the heart rate, reduce cortisol, and relieve anxiety.

- **Visualization.** Visualize standing at the edge of the ocean with your feet in the sand. With each wave toward shore, the water gently offers you its cleansing, purifying energy. As it recedes, it takes your negative or scattered energy with it. The ocean is strong and primordial; trust that it knows how to take care of you. You can do this almost anywhere.

- **Noticing the senses.** For growing anxiety or panic attacks in crowded city elevators or neighborly disagreements—or what have you—use the 3-3-3 method if you can: Find and name three things you can see and three you can hear, and then move three body parts.

- **Hydration.** Drink a glass of water; as you do so, visualize your body being soothed by nature's greatest gift. Feel the water alchemizing your emotions.

- **Connecting to place.** If you are in your favorite park or city street, become aware of each and every step you are taking. Feel yourself rooted to place and space; feel the cement holding you. For many of us city witches, feeling a sense of home is integral to our mental well-being and to making magic in a place. This is a good way of establishing a relationship connection to your city and learning to see it as an anchor and a support to you.

- **Carry a stone that absorbs your energy.** Put it in your pocket or your bag. Obsidian takes in all that fog and rids us of it.

....

- **Do something tactile and beautiful and alive.** Put on some music, take a bath, decorate an altar space, pull some tarot cards, journal, drink tea next to an open window, create art, exercise, dance, and just be silent with and aware of your joy and heartbeat. Let everything you don't need fade out of focus and away from your body. Making a space in your home—your bedroom if you live with roommates—that feels clean, comfortable, and sacred is so important. Think of the colors, the objects, the sounds, and the scents—e.g., a silk throw, a collection of seashells, the perfume of neroli that reminds you of your heritage, a gold painting that makes you feel safe—that can absorb negative energies and return you to yourself.

FEELING ENERGIES

Energy has many definitions, and it has many names (Prana, Chi, Ki, Ruah, life force). Different practices and cultures view or work with it differently, and that is beautiful.

You may or may not already work with energy, or maybe you "just sense it" without exactly being able to describe it. Energy is nebulous, eternal, hard to understand. We know it creates and destroys, reacts to being observed, and changes shapes. To me, it is an invisible or subatomic divine.

There are so many incredible resources on energy work, but to put it simply, you are already doing energy work. Every day you live. Everywhere you go. Cities are full of energy—from people, from transportation, from events, from feelings, from problems, and from things we cannot even see. All of this creates collective hum. Specific spaces can trigger different perceptions of energy.

For example, walking through the East End of London (where Jack the Ripper gained his noteriety and where his victims became just a sidebar), I couldn't help but feel its traumatic history toward sex workers—and how it has shaped history. Sure, there were a few fancy shops and things were different, but I *felt* the energy. It stays. It wants us to notice it.

Part of sensing energy isn't to reach toward a thing or person to feel them; it's learning to quiet or still your own energy or space to be receptive to what's around you. To do this, bring your awareness to your body, and to the space around your body.

Breathe deeply. Visualize your own energy becoming quiet. Become aware of the open space *around* you. Be still. Feel your own energy (you can rub your hands together to feel it and then start to shape a ball where it exists). Next, feel the border between your energy and the energy around you. Being aware of, and practicing tapping into, that sense will help you *feel* any space or person.

Feel weird in a room? Sense someone looking at you? Just *know* that a person is trustworthy? That's what you're working with. Notice these things when you're in a space, a city park, a crowded bus station, a creepy subway car at night, a museum in the afternoon. You may feel energized, tingly, drained, quieted, heavy, anxious, nauseous, angry, peaceful, softened, comforted, lustful, or even epiphanic.

SHIELDING YOURSELF FROM WILD, NEGATIVE, TOXIC, TIRED, OR FRANTIC ENERGIES

While "shielding" may have a negative connotation, it's not just about keeping yourself protected from a potential threat. It's about honoring your boundaries, celebrating your worth, and knowing when to give and receive energies. Have you ever had a day where you have had it *up to here* with bullshit? Your office is filled with jerks. There's political turmoil in the streets around you, and during protesting, you want to ensure you can sustain your action and hope. Or maybe the noises and crowds during the long walk home from the bus is the tipping point and you want to establish armor so you don't feel oversaturated and angry. How many times have you thought, "I *need* to get out of the city?" It's a valid way of feeling. We can take action.

- **Envision a luminous cocoon around your body.** Visualize spinning it as the silkworm does, from your center outward about ten feet around your body, covering your whole being and personal space in shimmering light. Or a dark cloud. Whatever feels right to you. Nothing can enter to harm you.

- **Raise energy.** Do this by rubbing your palms together, taking note of that heat and heaviness—energy—and begin to move your hands outward around you. In this situation, you have used your energy to create a shield. You can speak aloud something like, "I am protected from energies that harm me; I am only receptive to the safe, the luminous, and the good."

- **Wear a shield.** I have the Eye of Horus tattooed on my arm, which protects me from evil intentions, and I often wear an Italian mano cornuto or horn amulet around my neck. You can power your shield with an object, a stone, a tattoo, or a scroll inscribed with words of your choosing. Write it, slip it in your jacket, and know it's keeping the shield up around you.

- **Wear a glamour.** In many cities, people feel empowered to express themselves how they choose. Some cities are very receptive to playful fashion, and glamour witches will embrace this. If your 1990s brown or azure lipstick gives you strength, program it as a shield. Same for your jacket or the outfit "vibe" or archetype you're going for. Whenever you apply your look, speak its power aloud:

"This glamour protects me; as I move through the streets, I embody strength, dignity, and protection from negativity." There's nothing superficial about donning a look or channeling an archetype; you are awakening, celebrating, and powering up your energy through an idea realized. This is a spell and it is alive. You are the spell.

CHANNELING THE CITY:
A RITUAL WRITING PRACTICE FOR EXPLORING YOUR RELATIONSHIP TO A CITY

Each city has its own magic, and each, in its unique way, reminds me of my own magic. They've shown me trust and reminded me of self-reliance. They've shown me passion and ardor and desire, and they've taught me to be comfortable in my skin. They've shown me sacredness and reminded me to be still and to take in my surroundings.

I've found a few cities where the connection is deep. In New Orleans, for example, there's a part of me eternally lost in the glittering, dark streets. The music, the open embracing of magic, the mix of cultures, the history, and the resilience of its people all inspire me. There's something very Scorpionic about New Orleans: It willingly walks into the shadows and the liminal. It survives. Being there, I am asked to look beyond what I can see. I am asked to look at New Orleans' past and present and to learn about its future. I always come away more intuitive, more tuned-in, more alive. But it's also a city that can easily be defined by tourism narratives, and so as part of my connection to the city, I try to learn about it and listen to its people. That I often find myself calling on the lessons I've learned in New Orleans *is* city sacredness moving through me.

To prep us for all the rituals and practices ahead, begin thinking about how cities (your own or one you've visited) have enchanted, changed, inspired, and taught you (for better or for worse).

Now, there are many things we may use in our various magical practices—candles, tarot cards, crystals, divination techniques—but were we to have *none of them*, the magic we *do* have is in our self-understanding, intuition, and ability to connect with a space's energy. That's what we'll be honing here in this first writing experience—the feeling that a city can transform us and reveal truths to us.

You can do this with the city where you live, of course, but if you do plan on channeling a city you've visited (one that particularly haunts you, as if a part of you is still there, waiting for your return), sift through your memories, photos, and videos of it, and revisit it often. There's a connection for a reason.

Do you have a city that stays with you and reminds you of your own inner magic?

First, arrange a cleansed and quiet space where you can channel the city through memories, feelings, energies, and items. Light a single candle to signify this as a ritual act. When we light a candle, the space changes; it becomes sacred, intentional, *yours*. You may want to pull out clothing, knickknacks, decorations, or anything else garnered during the trip. Touch the items; let the colors and fabrics call you.

Close your eyes, breath in and out slowly until you feel receptive and malleable. Let yourself *become* the energy of the trip.

Journal Prompts: The City that Lives Within You

- Which city comes to mind?
- What about it floods your senses? Its colors? Its people? Its foods? Its architecture? Its city center?
- What memory asks to be remembered?
- What does the city say to you?
- What did you discover about yourself when you were there?
- How did the city make you feel about it and yourself?
- What part of yourself did you leave behind while there?
- What was the energy of the city that you picked up on the most? How did this energy affect you?
- Are there spirits or archetypes you identify with in this city?

If it is the city in which you live, or a city that shaped you, you can also use these prompts:

- What did it feel like when you moved here?
- Are you part of the narrative? What does it feel like to be part of this city's narrative?
- How does the city make you feel about it and yourself?
- Are you struggling to love or identify with your city?
- Are there parts of your city experience that still enchant and beguile you?
- What part of yourself did you develop and nurture here?
- What part of yourself did you shed here?
- What is the city's (or neighborhood's) energy in this very moment? How has that energy shifted? What can you learn from it? How is it affecting you?
- Are there spirits or archetypes you identify with in this city?

FEELING AND RAISING YOUR BEAUTIFUL, POWERFUL ENERGY

*Every*thing has an energy, including places; it's something you *feel*. Something you sense. Something that changes you. There are many methods of manipulating and using energy. Here, we will raise it with a simple practice—and this is something you can come back to over and over if you have little experience with energy.

Steady your breathing, find a moment of peace. Shut your eyes or keep your gaze soft. If you are in a public place, please don't shut your eyes. Rub your hands together and feel the heat; this is tangible, easy, and gives you physical focus. Feel the rising energy. You are simply calling forth your energy, not creating it. When you feel it, play with it. Hold both your hands out and cradle the energy field between them.

You can send this energy outward physically, you can visualize a space where the energy goes, you can use it to program an amulet or charm (to be worn or hung in the home) simply by holding it and stating your intention, you can put it into a crystal (to be held or displayed on an altar or in your home), and you can send love to your city in the form of your energy.

When you are working with energy, be intentional about what you are doing with it. If you are programming a charm or crystal with the energy of a space, don't be haphazard with it. Be specific and mindful of what you want and how you feel as you proceed.

CITY WITCHERY

CLEANSING YOUR SPACE AND PREPARING IT FOR SACRED EXPERIENCES

Some of the practices and rituals listed throughout this book take place within the home (like your apartment) Before engaging in ritual or any sort of sacred act (like journaling or visualization), it's a good idea to cleanse yourself *and* the space of any dull, stagnant, or harmful energies.

These energies can come from people's moods (this is called the "evil eye" or Malocchio in my practice), your own exhaustion, or the city's wild, fluctuating energy. You carry it with you when you come in and out, after all.

Clear your space by making a smoke or spray cleanse (see **What you'll need to work with this book, pp. 17**) for ingredients to use for burning. For small or not-well-ventilated apartments, I recommend a spray bottle cleanse.

AN EASY-TO-MAKE, APARTMENT-FRIENDLY, ENERGY-CLEANSING ELIXIR POWERED BY THE MOON

You'll Need:

- **LARGE BOWL** or **MASON JAR OF WATER**
- **HERBS** (especially those bought locally or those that are embraced by your ancestors or practice. I like to use rosemary for its cleansing properties or lavender for its soothing and healing scent) or organic essential oils. Try to ethically source your goods if possible and be mindful of pets and roommate allergies
- **A WATER-SAFE CRYSTAL** (optional). I use rose quartz to promote love in a space or clear quartz (within the water) to clear negative energies)
- **A FEW PINCHES OF SALT** (any salt will do; many use coarse or sea salt as it's often on hand, and some use black salt, which is said to absorb negative energies). Salt is often used in protective and cleansing acts
- **A SPRAY BOTTLE WITH AN ATOMIZER.** I like to use glass, but anything will do. You can also skip the bottle and keep the water in a jar! Simply use your fingers to spray the water; there's magic in your hands and movement

Let the water sit under the moonlight (see **Moon Water Magic pp. 86**) overnight to charge (it's probably safer if you do this on a windowsill or a back porch where it won't be disturbed). You may place a crystal within the water to infuse the water with it as well. Cover the jar or bowl so no dust or room-mates or furry familiars can get into it. When placing it under the moonlight, be intentional with it. Ask that the water be blessed and programmed to cleanse and purify your space.

You can speak this aloud (or, even better, write your own incantation):

May this water be blessed by the light of the moon, that it becomes as the moon is: luminous, divine, capable of the tides of change. May this water be used to cleanse, purify, and create harmony in my space.

Here's an outline for you to work with:

May this water he _____ by the light of the moon. May it become as the moon is: _____. May this water be used to __ __ in my space.

In the morning (I personally get the water whenever I wake up; some people need extra sleep and that's *okay*), collect the water and pour it (along with any herbs or other bits) into your bottle if you choose to use one. You can make a different mixture every week and when the seasons change.

If you have a small enough crystal, you can drop it in as well. Use this spray when the energy, air, or "traffic" becomes stuck, stagnant, or tiresome. I recommend opening a window and using this spray elixir in each room and space you inhabit, especially before a ritual or during journaling. You can even keep a smaller bottle near your front door with which to spray upon your being when coming in from outside.

Of course, any intentional act is enhanced with intentional words. If you recite an incantation every time you used the spray, or as you move through each room or through your front door, what would you say? What intention would you like to impart?

You may start with:

With this sacred water, this space becomes _____, free from _____, energized by _____.

"Roads are a record of those who have gone before."

—REBECCA SOLNIT, *Wanderlust: A History of Walking*

WANDER

LETTING YOUR
INTUITION LEAD YOU

WANDERING, WITH ALL OF ITS inherent energetic curiosity, can benefit any sort of city witch practice. Whether you are wandering your own city streets to forge a deeper relationship to it, or wandering another city during travel, the act of wandering alchemizes curiosity into creativity, energy, and self-growth.

My own wanderings have led to some incredible experiences, drinking in the energy and story and magic of each place. Meandering through the streets of Bath, the largest city in Somerset, England, (known for its Roman baths) I simply let myself get lost. As I passed by its picturesque Palladian buildings, I came across a sign etched with the words, "Sanitas per aquas," or "Health through water," words that followed me through my trip. Had I not let myself get lost, would I have found those words? I think not—and that is a kind of magic.

I reflected on how water figures into my own wellness and magical practices. I learned Minerva, the Roman goddess of wisdom, watched over the waters in Bath. In fact, according to Taking the Waters (see **Resources pp. 141**), it was said people would seek retribution and revenge through Minerva at the sacred springs of Bath by writing the name of their enemy and plunging it into the water. How absolutely delicious!

And so in my wanderings—sans map and Wi-Fi—I passed both upscale restaurants and fancy hotels and the remnants of ancient springs where magic took root. That energy stayed with me (especially as I am a water sign), and I used it to write poems and even a letter to Minerva myself, asking for wisdom.

Of course, I've also wandered through my own city, getting onto a free ferry to Governors Island, which is a 172-acre park full of hammock groves and sunflowers and bike paths in the middle of the water off of downtown Manhattan. But in my travels, I did some research. I found that in the 1500s, the Lenape made a home on the island, which was then called Pagganuck. The land, as we know, was stolen from them, but its energy and history remains, asking to be seen and acknowledged. How better can we move through a space—engaging its flora and fauna, using its footpaths to restore our wellness, or tapping into its energy for inspiration—than to truly know its name, its face, its blood?

There is a story behind every place, and those stories are there to teach us, to comfort us, to empower us. To remind us we are part of the woven fabric of time. To me, making magic isn't only about casting spells. It's about learning, growing, and sinking into the layers.

CAPTURE A SPACE'S ENERGY IN AN OBJECT

In my own sacred wandering practices, I bring (or find) an object, like a stone, that I program to absorb some of the energy of my journey. This is especially helpful if you are using a journey through a city as a pilgrimage to an ancestral place or wandering through the streets of a place where something powerful occurred.

If you want to retain and tap into that energy later—to write, to cast a spell, to design an altar—a stone is a good way to go. Simply carry it in your hand and visualize the energies it captures as you move. You may also wish to place it in a specific spot (a spot of grass, the sidewalk itself, in the center of a busy [but empty!] intersection) to absorb a space's energy for a moment.

For example, in Italy, I've captured the feeling of my ancestral homeland in a smooth, bowl-like seashell. I place it upon my altar with a bit of salt water in it when I want to ask for that space's energy—full of sunlight and the sea; the curious, awe-struck energy of that trip; and the Italian celebration of pleasure and experience.

When we are retaining energy like this, what we're really doing is using the object as a trigger. We know we've programmed a stone to hold the energy of a space; whenever we touch or hold or meditate with it, we are changed. The feeling is activiated. We have changed the object, and it has changed us.

NOTICING SYNCHRONICITIES

We are, as energetic beings, always at play—or collaborating with—the world around us. Most of the time, we live on cruise control, simply going through the motions (and that's okay! We sometimes need our feet on the ground). But city magic isn't just an action; it's also a state of being tuned in. Ears up. Eyes open.

The concept of synchronicities was explored by Carl Jung (founder of analytical psychology and an occult enthusiast) who posited two or more psycho-psychic occurrences had some deeper meaning, and they were not just simple coincidence. The idea is the great *everything*—the collective, the universe, whatever you call it—is stretching its hands out toward us, and we need to notice.

Throughout time, magical folk have always *noticed things*, meaningful coincidences and events that seem disconnected but then ultimately converging, begging for our attention. We may see numbers or objects, or we are reminded of something only to later see that something. Could it be clairvoyance? Could it be a message from some greater energy force? You decide. The only thing that matters is you pay attention.

A Practice: While wandering, take note of any repeated words, numbers, images, colors, names, things that happen after you think of them, or symbols. Do they remind you of something in a dream, something you saw or talked about yesterday, or something that's been on your mind? The wanderer is a free agent, receptive to the space around them, part of it, in communication with the untethered state that leads to epiphany.

LUMINOUS LOSTNESS:
CITY AS A REFLECTION OF SELF

Wandering allows us to notice things we wouldn't otherwise: the geometric shape of a building, a sign, a plaque, a street name (which may indicate some history), a park, a type of flower (What do its colors make you feel? What sort of flowers grow here?), the way the water gently trickles through a small park pond. Wandering may also have an energy that makes you feel a certain way.

In this practice, you will wander through the streets of a city, taking note of its energy, sounds, scents, and "languages" it speaks. If you are unable to physically move through a space or set yourself in a central location, you can absolutely visualize yourself moving through the streets, immerse yourself in old video footage, or conjure the feeling through photographs.

Materials
- A notebook or voice recorder
- A crystal, stone, or other item that can absorb energy

If you are in your own city, visit a city neighborhood that speaks to you—perhaps one you want to spend more time in, a space that calls out to you (like an art or university district), or a seaport or neighborhood that celebrates a particular culture. If you are visiting another city, try routing yourself by starting at the city center and moving outward or at the city's edge and moving inward.

Try not to let a map guide you, and check in with yourself on where and why you want to walk. What is calling you? Is it a particular park at the end of the road? The sounds of a crowd? The power of a protest or rally? The energy of academia or creativity or culture? The warmth of a tree-lined avenue? The flooding glow of lights from a street of pubs and galleries? A band playing in the street?

Follow what feels right and what calls out to you, and let your curiosity guide you. And above all, of course, your safety is a priority (especially for marginalized and femme-presenting folks).

Now, translate the magic. As you move through the space, take note of what you are drawn toward and why. Is it the sound or color? Is it an untranslatable energy that pulls you? Is it an intuitive magnetism? Write these into your city grimoire every time you come across a realization. Oftentimes, we travel in a blurred, take-it-all-in sort of tornado—and there's beauty in that. But here, we are tapping into our wandering and recording the sensations of it.

If you find yourself entranced by tall buildings, what is it about them that lures you? Is it the power and energy and connectedness to the sky? Can you feel the bigness of human creation in their architecture? Or are you fascinated by how different the transportation system is—bikes versus cars, for example? Why does this speak to you?

If the draw is hiding at the bend of a cobblestone road, is it the underbelly of a city (the faces in the dark, the strangeness, the off-the-beaten-path gems) that speaks to the psychic detective in you? Perhaps you want to know the city beneath all the glitz and glam. Perhaps these dark corners will teach you about yourself.

Or, perhaps, there are energies that *don't* appeal to you, streets where you feel uncomfortable or on edge. Take note of where they are and why. Are they streets or a neighborhood where, historically, a crime or trauma took place?

In your city grimoire, write these ideas down. It doesn't have to be in fully fleshed out sentences. Just get the feelings out. Make the connections.

What is this city trying to teach you?
What has it revealed to you about itself and yourself?

In wandering, we hone our intuition (by listening to it), we connect with energy around us (by allowing ourselves to feel it), and we let the city hold its mirror up before us. In its reflection, we see ourselves.

CONNECT

CONNECTING WITH YOUR CITY
THROUGH ITS HISTORY,
NATURE, AND ART

EVERY CITY, EVERY STREET, and every place (and even every room) has a heartbeat, and if you tune in, you can hear it. In cities, that beat is an eternal hum. It is the magic and the music of time and constant energy, almost as though past and present have folded into one. On the surface, a city appears to be one thing, but they are complex and layered. Cities are also made up of what we don't or can't see. Or what's not remembered anymore.

We can intuit a place's secrets and energies if we tune in to the current; the more you learn about a place, the deeper that connection gets. This can reveal yourself *to yourself* and deepen your experience of being alive and present, which, to me, *is the very essence of magic*. It can make you feel at home. It can give you purpose and drive and a sense of connectedness.

My life has always been grounded by a *tuned-in*-ness and a sense of place. Wherever I am, I feel my environment deeply (which is why changing houses or cities always shakes me up). Where joy hums, I sing. Where shadow clings and energetic imprints of sorrow linger, I feel that too. I bow humbly to the cycles of life and time.

Cities are multicultural, richly lived and loved places where people are born and bred and sculpt the ever-changing fabric of its story. Cities are life-changing places where others go to create themselves, to embrace their identities, to form new communities and find chosen families, and to seek access to the things they may have lacked before. But cities are also beasts. They can be painful places of lands that have been stolen, and where the heaviness of capitalism and gentrification take root. Fortunately, city magic can help us be more aware of how we can also make a space better.

Cities—in their myriad shapes, sizes, and personalities—are sacred places where magic *does* grow. In this chapter, we'll explore a few ways of connecting to a city: though its history, nature, and art.

CONNECTION THROUGH HISTORY

Honoring the Energies of the Past

Before Manhattan was colonized, it was all farmland and rolling hills. Its natural landscape was demolished, eventually making way for its grid system. And while it is easy to glamorize a city like New York—TV says it's all hailing cabs and drinking cosmopolitans and fighting for opportunities (*for certain people*)—the truth is, this was a green land belonging to Indigenous people whose stories ought not be forgotten. And it was also a place where immigrants came to create family and community and change.

There was a sprawling sheep meadow where the famous restaurant Tavern on the Green stands now. There's ancient bedrock in Central Park (sadly, so much of it was blasted away in the Park's design). Standing on that bedrock connects me to the primordial energy of our universe. And at the corner of 84th and Broadway, I can sense the ghosts of an old farmhouse where Edgar Allan Poe was said to have written "The Raven."

There is power and energy in history. When we tap into a space's stories and past, we feel the energy of time. Perhaps you may also want to tap into the spirit energies of a place; what better way than to know what memories a space holds, or what emotional imprints have been made?

A PRACTICE: Research the history of your city (or some portion of your city, like a neighborhood or a park) and visit it, if possible. Stand in the echo chamber of its history; try to sense it, feel it, transcend the now-ness of the city and tap into what it was before colonization and modernization.

Ask the energies if they are aware of—and if they *mind*—your presence, and see what your intuition or gut feeling picks up on.

How does learning about the history of a space change your relationship to it? How has its history led to the city's current identity? Is there a sense of good and hope where you stand? Is there a sense of dread and turmoil?

Connecting in this way is an act of magic, for magic is intuitive. Magic is being present. Magic is being aware of what exists underneath the surface. Magic is honoring cycle and time. Magic is curiosity and respect and gaining knowledge.

Write a poem or journal about the history of your city; read prose and poetry about the history of your city, especially from the voices you don't hear enough from.

CONNECTION THROUGH NATURE

*Green Portals: Magical Practices and Prompts to
Embrace City Green Spaces*

One of my deepest pleasures as a city witch is visiting a green space (a large park, botanical garden, community garden, or cemetery) that evokes that incredibly palpable sense of shifting energy.

In these spaces, we feel an invisible curtain has been drawn; suddenly, the sounds of the cityscape become muffled and distant. And yet, a city's green spaces *are* still part of the city; they're just quieter, more still, another hue.

Here's how we can work with those spaces:

EARTHING ALLOWS US TO GROUND OURSELVES AND FIND RESPITE FROM THE CHAOS, NOISE, AND WORKDAY STRESSORS

Earthing is the act of placing your skin upon the earth to feel its energy and to be healed and soothed by its electrons. *The Journal of Environmental and Public Health* found earthing can reduce blood pressure, heart rate, and stress levels, and spending time in it can even lessen pain and insomnia. Earthing is also a beautiful way of grounding; it can be done in any park, community garden, desert, lake, or green space.

Find a natural space that calls to you (or is simply nearest to where you spend most of your time) and get to know it. Find a favorite bench, rock, or nook and spend time with the trees, flowers, and bushes near it.

Simply breathe in and envision the energy of nature settling into your skin and then into your blood and bones, the essence of your being. Still yourself and tap into the layer between you and nature. Feel it dissolve. We are nature. We are one. Feeling this truth is a magical act.

CITY WITCHERY

A Practice: To ground yourself, place your feet firmly on the ground. Feel yourself anchoring to the ground, and then to what is below it, and what is below that, until you feel synced up to the earth's subterranean core. Visualize that connection and let yourself be grounded physically. Continue to breathe. This is especially useful if you are overwhelmed by work or a busy to-do list, are overstimulated easily by chronic illness or external triggers, or if you feel lonely.

Let the earth reaffirm you are held; let yourself be held. Tune in or out of the distant city buzz. You can simply *be*. Even if you're rushing around the city or grabbing a coffee, there are usually a few patches of grass or a tree you can stand beside. If you can't find grass or take off your shoes, simply place your hand upon a tree's bark. It can absolutely root you to the earth.

If you have a patio, shared roof space, stoop, or back garden, you can do this there as well for a quick dose of nature. Be present and feel the air surrounding your body.

DEVELOP A CONNECTION WITH THE FLORA AND FAUNA IN MEDITATION OR RITUAL

As a city dweller, it often feels you can go the whole day and not see a color that isn't silvery or synthetic. Although we should reframe the ways we see the city (buildings aren't bad and magic *does* exist in a city), a want for nature is natural. Seeing a tiny green weed grow through the grates and sidewalk cracks can be heart-tuggingly sweet, a reminder of resilience. That some things don't change.

You may learn of plants native to your region and seek them out in a park; or perhaps there is a flower or herb that's used in local cultural customs that you can learn about. Apothecaries, flower shops, occult shops, and botanical gardens often have this information and will be willing to share. The spirits of local flowers and grasses will root you to your place and may even ignite magical connectedness. Suddenly, the city isn't "just" cement or traffic; it is, too, a place of nature. And that nature lives alongside the things humans have made.

Flowers and trees can speak to us in specific ways. Perhaps you find yourself drawn to a lakeside weeping willow on the water's edge of your city (looking at you, Ithaca, New York); a small sidewalk garden commemorating a loss, tragedy, or significant city event; or a type of flower specific to a neighborhood culture. Each of these natural beauties offers us some insight—about itself, ourselves, and the space it grows in. Connect with it, learn about it, and develop a relationship with it. You'll never know when a specific flower or tree becomes a symbol of strength to you, or when hanging its picture in your sacred space will make you feel at home or in your power.

Find a kind of plant, flower, or tree in your local park, cemetery, or botanical garden that you can visit and spend time with. Bring your city grimoire; plants offer messages in ways we don't always notice. These may come as images, sensations, or flashes of wisdom.

MOON MAGIC FOR CITY DWELLERS

When the moon moves through one of the twelve astrological signs, the energy of that sign seems particularly resonant (you can easily track which sign the moon is in using an app like "The Moon" or "Moon Tracker"). As the moon changes signs, life's moods or hues change since each astrological sign offers different qualities and energies. You may feel it subtly or strongly, or you may want to tap into it for intentional reflection and cyclical magic. Below are some practices and prompts for city witches to use when the moon is in a given sign.

You can also apply these to your city travels (if you know, for example, the moon will be in three or four different signs during a trip).

When the moon is in Aries, it asks us to get physical, to take initiative, to tap into our feisty energy. This is a good time to start a community action group, use your voice to create change, or ideate around a show or event series that is open to the public. If you are living in a city with parks or near water, think about getting into the water or onto the trail and using the city's natural offerings to express your physicality and energy. If you feel rage or anxiety or frustration at systemic obstacles or personal issues—feel it and get it out of your body (maybe that's through sex or dance or a long run or song or whatever physical activity feels right to you). If you are traveling, now is the time to separate from the group, take a risk, get your body involved, and make the experience your own. The city calls. It is also the time to light a candle, take a deep breath, and envision the stress and madness of city life evaporating from your body.

When the moon is in Taurus, it asks us to find some time for self-pampering and beauty. Visit your city's botanical gardens, estates, or natural heritage sites (or simply take a stroll through the park) and luxuriate in having access to beauty. You can also visit the library (if it's particularly beautiful), the art gallery district, or a cute cocktail bar. Wherever there is a bit of beauty, even if it's a strip of lakeside, embrace it. This is the time to tap into your glamorous, indulgent side. Use color magic by buying a bouquet of flowers (Which colors inspire you? Yellow is great for creativity, while purple is wonderful for psychic energy and intuitive magic, for example). If you're traveling, you'll want to meditate on how a city's beauty inspires you. For example, is there something about its architecture that speaks to your creative side? Redesign your altar so it inspires you (see **Altars and Shrines pp. 80**).

When the moon is in Gemini, it asks us to tap into our outgoing, curious nature and to truly connect with others. This is the time to spark a conversation with someone new at a city-focused Meetup group (try your local city history group), with museum or city tour group, or during a pub trivia night. If you have a local occult shop, see if they have any events or excursions, and strike up a conversation with someone. Bring a friend if you feel more comfortable, and see if you can tap into curious extroversion. Learn, ask questions, share ideas, and bond over city experiences. If you're traveling, you may want to strike up conversation in another language (don't be shy!) or get into a deep chat with a local about their city. It's also a great time to ritualistically journal. Look at the duality of your city; ponder what it offers and how it can change, or look at what its history is versus what its current personality is (see **Ritual Journaling pp. 77**).

When the moon is in Cancer, the sign of the moon itself, it asks us to nest, to explore our domestic selves, and to make our homes into a sanctuary away from the city. How can you create a cleansing, safe space away from the wildness of the city within your home? This is a time to tend to an altar space, to bring the sacred in, to shop for plants or crystals or books that will make your space feel safe and inspired. Wander though thrift shops, sift through (and also donate to!) the Salvation Army, and find natural artifacts that speak to your home altar. This could be a time to press leaves or gather salt water from the sea or ask the earth if you can take a stone home for your hearth, windowsill, or altar space. It is also a time to tap into the sensitivity of your city, to understand the community's needs (through community forums or local fundraisers) and offer both support and a safe space in yourself. If you are traveling, it's a good time to feel your feelings in a new or foreign place—to discover yourself as you move through a new space. Run a self-care bath or take a hot shower and envision a protective, shimmering field surrounding your body, dissolving all negative energies from outside (see **Washroom Magic pp. 82**).

When the moon is in Leo, it asks us to embrace glamour, to step into the city as our more provocative, glamour selves. This may be a time to get dolled up and glamour passersby with your style and boldness. The anonymity of most cities allows us to play with this dressed-up identity; you can be whoever you want to be, channel whatever you want to channel. It's also a time to share love, compliment people, and offer your open, generous energy to causes and events. It may be a time to gather your friends for a night of cooking and good conversation; ask them to set an intention and to call on fiery, confident energy to make magic happen. If you are traveling, allow yourself a night of fun—dress up, dance, or meet with some locals and allow yourself to be immersed in conversation and new ideas. There is magic in letting go and calling on the divine energy of celebration and self-love. How does the city bring out the joy, confidence, and love in you? Journal about the hotspots in the city that inspire you most.

When the moon is in Virgo, it asks us to reevaluate what is working in our city lives. Are we taking the best mode of transport to work? Is there a quicker or more economic option? Are we living with roommates or in a building that feels unsafe or unwelcoming? If so, how can we make a plan to leave or break a lease? Are we being smart with our city spending habits? And if not, where can we afford to indulge while reconfiguring some other area? Virgo is about the details--but this doesn't mean we need to shame ourselves or get down on our current situation. It does mean, however, that we need to reframe what works. Are we allowing ourselves time to see the sites and experience what the city offers, or are we getting complacent? Are there free museum nights, for example, we can patronize to save money and still have experiences? Is there a way to better care for our health (jogging through a local park or accessing low-cost community health resources) while experiencing the cityscape? This is a time to list everything you want and everything that needs to be reframed and rewired. It's a time that asks us not to judge or be critical of those around us, too, and to instead ask how we can help. Be ready to embrace the mighty power of decluttering—light a few candles, throw out your trash, and sweep the old energy out (think of it as a magical Marie Kondo ritual).

When the moon is in Libra, it is the sign of diplomacy, justice, and balance. For a city witch, that means getting involved with community and seeking justice for those who can't seek it for themselves. Cities are places where things happen, where many of us have access to local leaders through forums and rallies. If it's safe for you, and if you're able to use your voice for the good of others, the moon in this sign asks for a commitment to showing up. Perhaps this means a donation or volunteering for a local shelter, taking part in a community petition to benefit LGBTQIA+ (Lesbian, Gay, Bisexual, Transgender, Queer, Intersex, Asexual+), the disabled community, or BIPOC (Black, Indigenous, and People of Color), or simply offering your friends support. The magic is you are putting your good and altruistic energy out there to transform your city and help the people within it (see **Resources pp. 141, for books that can inspire you**). It's a good time to gather strength and armor up so you can use your good to help others.

 When the moon is in Scorpio, it is the sign of birth, death, and transformation. Though Scorpio energy is oft-misunderstood (yours truly is a Scorpio!), the misunderstanding is for a reason. Scorpio energy is concerned with the depths, with transmuting pain into meaning, and with the grotesque things society hides from. Pain cannot be hidden or ignored, lest it grows. When the moon is in Scorpio, it is a time to visit the cemetery and to contemplate on life and death, to grieve, to stand beside witness trees that have bloomed from death. It is time to set a candle out for the dead and speak to your loved ones. It is time to read the poetry of dead poets who lived or died in your city—and to feel their depths. It is time to research the subterranean or the spooky, darker history of your city. Visit the local library and find records of what stood in your apartment's plot of land. From catacombs to ghost stories, there's much to be gained from the chthonic, from what we cannot see, from the cycle of time. What does this darkness teach you? How does it deepen your relationship to your space? How can we use grief and pain—perhaps for our city's losses—to grow or start anew? If you are traveling, do a search for "dark tourism" in your area or use a site like Atlas Obscura to find spaces that are off the beaten path. How is your city a phoenix, and how is it a ghost? (see **Shadow Working Your City pp. 110**).

When the moon is in Sagittarius, it asks us to follow our impulses and let go. All that fiery energy can inspire us to try new things, eat new foods, visit new places, and buy a one-way plane ticket. While it's important to keep yourself safe, now's the best time to travel, to unleash your inner wanderer, and to let go of the attachments that can keep us stagnant. Disappear into a crowd, visit a neighborhood you've never been to, or sign up for a pub crawl. If you are traveling, this is the time to detach yourself from set itineraries and to get lost in the energy of place and transportation. For example, how does being on an airplane flying over sprawling cities make you feel, or how does a long train ride through the city inspire you? How does it differ from home, and how does that feed your hunger for life? And because Sag has a tendency toward wanderlust, perhaps this is *the* time to tap yourself into the here and now by purposely tuning into the music of the city. Situate yourself on a porch, a table in the middle of a square, or a park bench and listen. Listen to everything—the buses and the birds, the footsteps and the fuss. This is a presentness practice and at the core of it is you using all that energy to fire up your magic.

When the moon is in Capricorn, you'll want to focus on work. Now's the time to dig into your big ideas and dreams for projects. Want to finish a poetry collection? Want to start growing a herb garden? Want to talk to your boss about a raise? Capricorn says, "let's go." It's also the time to do "inner work," work that asks you to remove the toxic garbage from your life. Work that aligns your values and your vision. Work that brings friends together. Work that feels good and right and beautiful. This could be deepening your spiritual practice, your workout regimen, your art practice. This is the time to shine a light on what brings you joy, focus, and fulfillment. Find a career coach or seek out a career-focused Meetup group. It may be a good time to start a ritual journaling practice.

When the moon is in Aquarius, you want to delve into matters of outer space, higher realms, and the ideascape. Detach yourself from the physical and material, and embrace the intellectual; ideate, dream big, use technology for change, ask yourself what expansion looks like. It's also the time to visit places of power, to venture off the path most commonly taken, to look at statues, monuments, and buildings of antiquity, and to understand their place in the scheme of life. Does your city have an observatory? Is there a roof or high point upon which you can daydream? Is there a tour of little-known neighborhoods? Go to where the strange lurks. Your heart will bloom, and your mind will be nourished.

 When the moon is in Pisces, you have permission to daydream. We're talking colossal dreamscape energy here—fill your space with flowers and fall asleep with the light pouring on your face. Use your favorite herbal or lushy remedy and get to work on a painting, poem, or love letter to someone you haven't spoken to in a while. Dive into the feelings you've been avoiding. Visit gardens and beautiful buildings, attend the theatre and see an experimental show, attend an acoustic sidewalk performance, get lost in the streets at night. Fill your heart with the luminous and the vulnerable and the fantasy.

CITY WITCHERY

CONNECTING THROUGH ART

Architecture, Art and Poetry

"Humanity leaves immortal echoes through its history using the media of language, art, knowledge, and architecture. . . . These echoes are not simply viewed in retrospect; they are primary to our time and define our civilization at any given moment, justifying our very sense of being human."

— **VIKAS SHAH MBE**

In Barcelona, Antoni Gaudí's architecture sings of nature and geometry. In Santa Fe, the adobe brick buildings root people to earth and warmth.

Architecture tells stories we so often ignore because we don't look up or we aren't prompted to look closely. We can take our cities for granted, looking to get home or to work, rather than peering around us at the glaring proof of mankind.

Walking through doorways or getting into an elevator, we are surrounded by the living, breathing past of a city—and by the beliefs and ideas people held. That energy lingers, though, which is why buildings or statues honoring evil people or painful parts of history are often dismantled. Some buildings are beautiful; others are a direct result of oppressive regimes or an attempt at homogenizing society.

Architecture can tell us about beliefs held by the builders, like myths and superstitions, religion and power structures. In New York City, buildings *still* skip the thirteenth floor, as the number "13" is considered unlucky. In Palermo, Sicily, grotesques haunt onlookers from Baroque structures, their wild eyes reminding us that dark forces are ever-present, and they must be scared away. Then there are the meaningful flourishes we may miss if we aren't looking: In Vermont, for example, witch windows are found in nineteenth-century homes; bizarrely, they're turned on an angle—so witches couldn't fly into them, of course. In New Orleans, there are several Gates of Guinee—Guinee being a liminal passing-by space in the underworld in Louisiana Voodoo—where, if you were to encounter them, you'd pay your respects.

In a sense, architecture is poetry. Its beauty is in how it translates the essence of its city, its maker, its time. This is its language, its line breaks, its ability to be many things at once.

What are the architectural styles and flourishes in your city?
What do they say about local culture, religion, and how your city has changed?
How does the energy shift when older structures sit beside modern buildings?
What makes you feel uneasy, and what inspires you?

A Practice: Write a poem about a building. Note its windows, its doorways, its arches, its gargoyles, its colors, its smallness or massiveness. Note how it fits into the cityscape around it. *What does it say to you? If you were to name the building, what would be its name, its sun sign, its secrets, its ego, its type of magic?*

CONJURING YOUR CITY'S SPIRIT: OF POETRY AND CREATIVITY

Like spirits of a city, the poets of yesterday linger. Think of John Keats roaming, all sensitive and brilliant, reciting poetry in London's Hampstead Heath (or in Rome near the Spanish Steps). Think of Gwendolyn Brooks writing about urban experiences in Chicago. Think of Emma Lazarus who wrote

"The New Colossus," which sits at the Statue of Liberty. Think of Nadia Tueni, a Beirut-born and educated poet who examined her home country of Lebanon in her works. These poets and their art glitter as ghosts through the city's streets, ever-present, reminding us art's legacy and power.

Which poets haunt your city (or nearby cities)?
Which poets haunt the cities you travel to?

Look, poetry is not all sunlight on the moors. I also think of today's poets—I, myself, one of them—writing from cities the world over, crafting words of immigration, culture, class, and the body. They are engaging the city's stories.

"There is this energy and aggression and speed in a city that lends itself to poetry. We are surrounded by language, whether it's place names, digital signs, advertising hoardings, or the voices of market traders—it's everywhere. Cities are built with language," East London-based poet Tom Chivers told the Guardian.

One of the deepest ways to experience a city's energy is to tap into its layers of time and its creative works. Find your city's poets of the past and read their work aloud as you sit in parks. Find their homes or places they were known to write. Write your own poetry by candlelight, calling in your city poets to join you—as muse, as inspiration, as guide. Host a salon or reading night with friends; notice the way the energy shifts when you all call upon a poet or writer from history.

Art in general is a way of understanding the city in which it was made. So if paintings speak to you, or if music speaks to you, find your city's creators and spend time with them. Witnessing their work is a sort of conjuring; I especially encourage you to seek out the poets who were little known or forgotten. Give them a voice again and invite them into your creative environment. Erect an altar to a poet or creator, light a single candle for each poet you work with, and call their energy to your space.

I call on the energy of [insert local poet's name] in honor and openness.
I channel your poetics, your creativity, your vision.

Note the words, colors, feelings, and even images that come up. Take time to work with their energies; watch how you change and how your vision of the city changes. Write.

How does your own poetry morph when you call a creative energy, archetype, or spirit into your space? How does their work change the way you see your own city? If you are traveling, who are the poets that haunt your tourist spaces? What does it feel like to read their words, look upon their art, or remember their deeds?

LIBRARY BIBLIOMANCY: FEELING THE POWER OF THE CITY IN ITS STACKS

Libraries are places of potency and power; they are the physical custodians of time and idea. They hold the records, information, and stories that reflect the human condition. In many ways, it's a temple, both physically (the earth it stands on) and symbolically (its ideas).

In your library, you will conduct a bibliomancy ritual, which is the use of books for divination and insight. Bibliomancy directs us to a page or a line in a text for wisdom and help; it embraces mysterious forces. Perhaps, it's the author themself who shows up. Maybe it's some other universal current that does. Regardless, it offers a chance to reflect.

For this ritual, you'll find a specific book that speaks to you. You may want to find a holy text or a book of poetry by a poet born in your city.

Take deep breaths; feel yourself become receptive. Connect with the energy of the library—and its years of wisdom—and let the book fall open to any page. Let your fingertip fall upon a passage, with eyes closed.

What did it tell you?
What did you learn?

A TWELVE-LINE POEM
ABOUT YOUR CITY

Poems are spells because we can manifest, banish, or conjure as we write them—the creative energy itself feeding the intent. Poetry speaks through colors and moods. Poetry can translate and detail memory and trauma and place. Poetry allows us to play in the space of vision and imagination, to encode intent in language. A poetry practice asks us to create that which cannot be created by anyone else—which is the essence of power.

It's the way we can express the most liminal, the most complex, the most difficult, and the most beautiful things about a place and the people within it.

In this twelve-line poem, you will write about your city in a way no one has ever done before. This is an act of devotion.

THE FIRST THREE LINES
Describe your city in color, shape, or mood

_____

THE NEXT THREE LINES
Describe the way it makes you feel

_____

THE NEXT THREE LINES
Describe an aspect of its most telling, complex history

_____

THE FINAL THREE LINES
Describe what you want for it in the future.

CONJURE

CREATING A MAGICAL
HOME ENVIRONMENT, *OR* A GUIDE
FOR THE APARTMENT WITCH

N THIS SECTION, WE'RE EXPLORING the various ways we can merge the sacred and the mundane, and reframing our ideas of what is "allowed" to be magical.

The idea that magic is only for those with access to nature and the silent, dark sky is classist, reductive, and unrealistic. Cottages and herb gardens are splendid, but cities are often seen as antithetical to magic.

Cities, though they certainly offer their own kinds of nature, are densely settled and generally very busy. This has somehow led to an idea that city magic (and its twin, apartment magic) is less glamorous or messy.

But inside of small apartments in cities all over the world, witches gather. We make sacred potlucks with friends in cramped kitchens; we huddle together on tiny fire escapes to light a candle and pray to a lost loved one; we get community groups together to raise money for a cause or run a poetry magazine or offer one another tarot readings. Cities bring people together; it's all about numbers. There are simply more people, more neighbors, more communities, more witches.

There's a very specific city-dweller energy you can *feel* in cities and apartments. In some of my friends' homes, it's palpably magical and cozy and warm and loving. Recently, I spent time with my friend Denise in her enchanting backyard in Brooklyn; we sat under autumn's falling golden leaves with twinkling lights strung over our heads, the wires being pulled through her bedroom window. We talked about how city spaces can feel so hard to adjust to—like they're someone *else's* place, how a space can be loved into becoming a home, and how moving often is so normal and yet so sad.

"The spaces in which we have suffered from solitude, enjoyed, desired . . . remain indelible within us," writes Gaston Bachelard in *The Poetics of Space*. Our homes are ever present, almost haunting us, following us around in daydreams and in sleep. We can mark our lives in *befores* and *afters* when we move to cities or travel to cities or experience big life moments in our cities.

And so, even if we move every so often to avoid raised rents, or even if we are constantly barraged by the energies of transient neighbors, we have a call to create a home that feels good and safe and magical. Our spaces shape our lives.

In city apartments, we often have to keep our voices down, or we can't walk heavily, or we have to burn candles very carefully. But these are our homes; they may be inconvenient and stuffy and loud, but that makes them no less capable of sacredness! As my close strega friend Andi says, apartments remind us of a witch's cottage in the way only a small space can—it holds *so much* energy.

If you live in a city, this is the energy that surrounds you too.

What sort of magic does your space hold?
What sort of magic do you wish it held?

I've lived in all sorts of apartments and in all sorts of setups all over New York City. I've rented bedrooms with and without windows, slept in rooms overlooking a highway and rooms overlooking a garden. I've lived in apartments with partners, with a roommate, and with several roommates.

I've lived in apartments that felt light and airy and good, and apartments that felt chaotic and sad. Some of the best apartment experiences I've had were in spaces that were small and cluttered and inconveniently located because the energy was aligned and I used my space in a way that felt sacred and inspiring.

In each of my apartments, I've thought of all the people who came before me and sat in between my four walls, feeling and dreaming and creating. What were

their struggles? What were their wins? What did they have to do to get here? What happened to them? I think of how the layers of time in older buildings and well-worn rooms contain remnants and memories of eras before us. I think of how cities are magnets to those who want a change, who want an opportunity; who have struggled, who have assimilated; who have hoped for their children, who have made art; who have gone to spaces where they could make change.

From here on, I invite you to sense and touch and acknowledge those layers of memory and time, and I invite you to acknowledge the not-so-poetic truths about

CONJURE

apartments and city life. City living often (not always, of course; it depends on where you live and the nature of a given city) means roommates and small spaces. For many of us, it means rushing through life, sharing crowded train space, lugging our groceries onto buses, and feeling mentally overstimulated. It can mean being inundated with disparate energies and contending with sounds and scents and living space structures that are complicated.

The truth is, while our non city-dwelling friends likely have their own very valid limitations to contend with, they do have more physical space in which to move, to breath, and to think. In the city, all of that is at a premium. So we do what we can, for *we must*. City magic requires mental focus and compartmentalizing, but it also asks us to tap into our own inner power. When you can't always rely on a silent night alone or an elaborate garden altar to do some of the heavy lifting for you, you've got to be in close contact with your inner voice. You can do that.

The following rituals, practices, and prompts can be utilized in your own space. Their aim is to get you comfortable with seeing your home as a place of magic and to root you to a sense of place. I believe that spending time with your space unfurls its layers and can make it feel like home (which is especially potent if you move around a lot as many city dwellers do). We all need roots.

This section can also be paired down and adapted if you are traveling and staying in other rooms in other cities.

SECRET APARTMENT MAGIC

If you live with roommates, it's likely quite challenging to conduct an elaborate ritual in your shared space or take over the kitchen to create brews and elixirs. If you've got a witchy roommate or partner (and I suspect many of you may), then you may find it a bit easier. Still, having time and space—*alone*—is key.

Regardless of your situation, these below practices will come in handy for you as they are designed to infuse your home with intention, creativity, attention to the natural world, and purpose on a regular basis.

I've also included, where applicable, opportunities to use apartment magic while traveling and staying in a hotel or homestay.

Objects of Enchantment

Your entire home is a conduit of your magic intention. It is a space that exists both in the real world and the world of dreams and memories and futures yet to happen. It is a world outside of time, in some ways, and contains the potential of that which presides within it.

Your space is itself capable of conducting magic, and it can be done incognito (if you cannot openly practice magic or if you simply want to maintain a sacred household full of magic at every turn) by being full of enchanted objects. We can use objects, symbols, and reminders, or we can enchant (or charge, or program) them with a specific energy. For example, I use a painting of a skull on the way to my bedroom as a reminder of the importance of embracing life even in darkness. As a chronically ill person, passing by the art helps me when I have down days. The art isn't enchanted, but it serves a magical purpose nonetheless since I've decided *when I see it, a shift occurs.*

I also have a large shell to collect coins in; the shell is specifically enchanted to generate abundance every time a coin is collected. To enchant an object, you'll want to gather your energy by holding the object and infusing it with your energy and intent. State your intent aloud, or whisper it into the object. You can use the full moon to kick up your programming potency. Whatever you do, just make sure you are focused and clear on your intent and energy with each and every object.

In a home of magic, everything is what it is—and more. Enchanted energy hums from corners and sings on bookshelves, drenching your home in constant beams of benefic energy. Your citrine sitting on the windowsill is a conduit for creative energy. Your favorite ceramic mug offers healing. Your neroli perfume brings you confidence. And your doorway is a portal to safety and security on days when you feel anything but.

FOR TRAVELERS: If you are traveling and staying in a space temporarily, you can firstly enchant any object to keep you safe on your journey (see **A Ritual and Incantation for Safe Travels pp. 135**). You can also enchant your pillow to provide energy and deep sleep, or a crystal to keep you shielded from the energies of the space you are in.

Windowsill Wishes

If you have a plant or if you can get a new plant (particularly at the seedling stage), place a note of wish and manifestation beneath its pot as it grows (no one has to know it's there). With the nourishment and growth of the plant, so, too, will our desires be tended to by the sun and universe. You can replace or refocus the wish with each new moon.

FOR TRAVELERS: If you are traveling and don't have a plant, pick up a small candle and keep a piece of paper beneath it—it should be something you'd like to wish for during your stay in whatever city you are in. The fire will power up your wish. You can also call in the guardian of whatever city you are in.

Mirror Magic

Need a dose of magic in a pinch? Stand before your mirror and acknowledge yourself and your magic. Store a magically charged lip balm or lip color in the mirror cabinet to be applied when in need of magic. To do this, you can take a few deep breaths, light a candle to pull in energy, and charge any object with your intent.

Glamouring yourself is a way of saying, *I am capable of transformation*. This is an excellent tip for travelers, as well, as this magic is less about the mirror and more about your enchanted lip balm or makeup.

Sacred Sigils

From the Latin "Sigillum," meaning *seal*, or Hebrew's "segula", meaning *magic word*, sigils are magical symbols that carry tremendous energy and power. They are uniquely created from words or phases and every witch has a different method for creating them—well worth looking into (see **Resources pp. 141**, for guides to creating sigils).

Sigils are created from the letters in a word or phrase, but they can be embellished with dots, lines, and even other symbols (I like to use a constellation-like pattern that represents the zodiac if I'm trying to pull in a certain quality or energy). The point isn't to create a beautiful image but rather to represent an idea and a desired outcome.

Write your intent on a piece of paper in a word or phrase. This may be something like, "This space is safe and sacred." A common method is to strike out the vowels and any repeated letters. From what remains, use the letters to create your sigil. The *s* may be your starting point, through which you draw the *p*. Place the letters on top of and next to one another, paying attention to where you are putting them, and keeping your energy focused on the intention. Essentially, you are building your idea down into a form to be drawn and used. I like to draw sigils in chalk under my sofa, shelves, or bed. You can draw them into your food, carve them onto the wall with your fingertip, or write them on a piece of paper that you carry with you. There is a certain magic in forgetting they are there, doing your bidding.

FOR TRAVELERS: If you are traveling, drawing a safety sigil and hiding it under your bed or keeping it on your windowsill or door is a wise idea.

Consecrated Creations

There is nothing more magical than the process of creation itself; in making art, you are giving shape to your breath, touch, and psyche. You are creating from nothing.

If you can get your hands on a clay sculpting kit, some paint, and a canvas, or a candle-making kit (most of these can be found on Etsy for under $50

USD) you can create your own magical home decor and altar items. Use color to guide you; which colors brings inspiration? Which color is associated to an archetype or goddess you work with? Which color is associated with the element you work with most? Which color brings in the energy of calm or love? If you are painting or sculpting, draw or carve a sigil lightly, and then cover it in color. If you are making a candle, carve a sigil into its wax as it dries. This is a beautiful way to use your energy and create something that lives in and nourishes your space.

These creations are the containers of your innate divinity, the shape of our cosmic channeling; when set upon your space, they build layers in our homes—making our space more ours, more potent, more able to hold space for our magic.

RITUAL JOURNALING:
WRITING WITH INTENTIONALITY

If you read my book, *The Magical Writing Grimoire*, you're probably already familiar with my ideas of writing as a magical act. If you're not, in a nutshell, I believe language allows us to give shape to the liminal spaces we inhabit, sense, and know. Writing frees us and helps us connect to our divinity. Through words, we create something from nothing—the very essence of magic.

CRYSTALS FOR CITY WITCHES

I use crystals as *symbols* of certain energies and feelings, and I believe it is completely valid to associate certain crystals with specific feelings—even if it's not aligned with the "traditional" association. You may want to use a few crystals in your city ritual work, or around your space, according to their energies below.

CLEAR QUARTZ

cleanses and heals

OBSIDIAN

protects against negativity

AQUAMARINE

helps to express feelings and transform you

ROSE QUARTZ

self love

AMETHYST

increases intuition

LABRADORITE

self-discovery and wisdom

SMOKEY QUARTZ

relieves heaviness, anxiety

HEMATITE

grounds and focuses

SELENITE

removes energy blocks and walls; cleanses other crystals

In a ritualized journaling practice, we make space for our truth, a space that can be opened and then closed. The page has the strength and the love to hold your wounds, demons, secrets, and wishes; and if you come to it with honesty, it won't let you down. I recommend you use a journal to document your feelings, experiences, results, and realizations—especially those that relate to the offerings and ideas in this very book.

A journaling ritual may also be a great idea if you are new to a city and want to start understanding how you are feeling about it. Bring it to bars, cafés, museums, anywhere else that piques your interest. You'd be surprised at how beneficial the *process* of writing can be; it's not just about completing a journal entry or having an aha moment! It's about the discovery, and the long-term and quiet transformation that happens when you return to the page (and yourself). To write ritually, you need to create an atmosphere that makes it sacred. Rather than just writing, you'll:

- Use your city grimoire (a dedicated journal) so all of your thoughts are in one place.

  ....

- If you are home, cleanse your space, light a candle, and call upon guardians, angels, deities, archetypes, or your higher self; it can be especially helpful to write near you altar, but the beauty of this is you can do it anywhere.

  ....

- Take a deep breath and let yourself write—uncensored, without attention to craft or literary detail, led by complete rawness and honesty.

  ....

- There are many ways to journal effectively. When stuck, I recommend letting your subconscious onto the page by leading with stream of conscious writing—jotting down words, feelings, images and flashes of thought as they come, even if they make no sense. The words you write have power, so be mindful as you write them. Each letter, each phrase, carries weight.

  ....

- Close out the space by snuffing your candle; close your journal by envisioning the space itself closing, and turn the energetic "off switch" on the session. It's a good idea to ground after this and seek self-care (take a bath, drink water, stretch, dance) as you enter back into the material and physical world.

ALTARS AND SHRINES: THE PERMANENT, THE TEMPORARY, THE PORTABLE, AND THE ONES FOR DAYS IN BED

The altar is the witch's workspace. It is a diorama, a tableau, a moment that lasts forever; it tells a story, or many stories. It captures the magic of you, its flames burn bright for an idea or a wish or a goal. It is the many small pieces of your soul converging with the elements. And it can be anything you want it to be.

Growing up, I didn't have the money for tools, and although I'd borrowed books about witchcraft from the library, I could never get my hands on an athame or a chalice. No one had encouraged me to use a butter knife, or to adapt as I saw fit. I was young, and so desperately wanted to make magic "correctly." This led me down paths of doubt, leaving me to abandon my inner magic and questiong the rigidity of belief and path.

As I got older, I learned altars were about what mattered to you. They were intuitive. My grandmother was a tiny Sicilian woman. A devout Catholic who seemingly practiced benedicaria (a kind of Italian folk magic). My memories of her in her 90s are entangled with memories of altars and shrines—erected over the television, on little shelves, and in corners—all covered in embroidered cloth doilies, candles, images of the saints, tiny statuettes, crucifixion triptychs, figurines, vials, relics, holy water collected in old cola bottles (and taped over with pictures of Jesus or Mary).

I can evoke the scent of their home when I think back on these altars; their presence had a lasting effect on me. I can smell perfume, something dry and old, incense, the South Jersey air—a specific mix of *something* and trees. It has all become mythology to me.

And upon the altars were scrolls—tiny scrolls, etched with prayers and blessings, wishes, and words in both Sicilian and in English. She'd slip the scrolls in between statues of saints and figurines, or roll them up under hanging rosaries. Today, scrolls figure prominently into my magic, and you'll always find them on my altars.

So, the question is: What is important to *you*? Devote an altar to that. Many people keep one or two altars—or even more— in their homes, usually serving different purposes.

There may be a permanent general altar used to display sacred objects, tarot cards, and candles where *every* spell or ritual is conducted. Some people keep out-in-the-open-altars that may or may not appear magical and spiritual in nature; they may use a prominent shelf in the living room or have a small magical station in their kitchen. I have one myself—my literary altar. My windowsill has become my permanent literary altar, which looks otherwise like a windowsill of books with a few too many knickknacks. This is where I place my own books, as well as my favorite books, which I rotate in and out. This space is adorned in crystals, statues, stones, shells, and plants—objects of muse and beauty and the earth—which always figure prominently into my work.

There is always a single white candle upon this altar, lit only when I write (and I often write next to it). The altar is enchanted by all four classical elements (earth, wind, fire, and water) and I like to imagine the elements are feeding my creative and literary work. From the outside, this literary altar may seem purely decorative—but I know its true purposes: magic! I didn't realize it was becoming a permanent fixture until I started returning to it, magnetized. In a way, perhaps it erected itself. Perhaps things have a way of knowing when they should stick around.

You may also have a temporary altar dedicated to, say, ancestral work. This may contain family or place photographs, maps, or items from your homeland. It may be a space where you speak in another language (and you should feel very encouraged to make your magic multilingual if you speak more than one language!). The ancestral altar may be erected during a certain season, when you need to call on or heal the ancestral bond, or as devotion for a family member's birthday. It is generally private (and can be kept on a bookshelf, on the dresser in your room, or even in a closet shelf) if you live with others.

WASHROOM MAGIC: RITUAL SHOWERS AND CLEANSING PRACTICES

To have the sea or a deep blue lake at your disposal would be a dream. Just to dip your feet into its depths—or to smooth your hands over its surface, writing words of wishes into ripples—would be a delight. But water is water, and all water is connected, part of the same life-giving divine energy.

"But is bathing really that magical?" you may ask. Yes! In an apartment, it's a sacred practice available to many of us. Don't forget that simply immersing yourself in water *is* enough. Magic isn't only made in elaborate ritual or through spell work; it's also made by working with elements in the way you can. Letting the water cleanse you. Letting its energy merge with yours. Being in conversation with the primordial elixir of life.

Embrace this ritual when you've had a particularly tough day running around or dealing with chaotic energy. On the other hand, a bathing ritual is also a great way to spend quality time *with* your space and to connect with its soothing and comforting spirit.

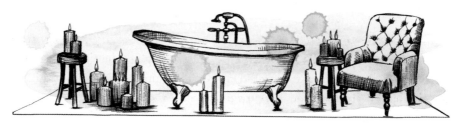

A Ritual Bath Recipe:

- Cleanse and prepare your space (with moon water or herbs); if this means asking to have the bathroom undisturbed for thirty to sixty minutes, try to do so. Ready the space so it feels inviting and sacred. You may burn some incense or sprinkle in some essential oils (I love lavender, rosemary, or rose) to the water as it runs warm (you can do this in the shower as well).

- If you have access to eucalyptus, you can hang it around your shower nozzle to fill the space with a natural, clean scent. You can decorate your bathtub with seashells or crystals on the rim to evoke a sense of nature and magic.

- Light a candle. Meditate on its illumination. Be grateful it offers you a chance to illuminate your intention.

- Write and speak an incantation before stepping into the water (see below). Be intentional and clear—ask for what you want.

- Step into the shower or bath or simply cleanse your hands in a bowl of water. Focus on your breath as you experience being alive. You may also want to sing along to music, using your breath to play with the sound.

The incantation may read something like:

May this water purify my body and cleanse my mind and spirit of any negative or limiting energies. As I cleanse my body, all that I do not need to

*carry vanishes down the drain. When I step out, I will be anew—full of light
and possibility.*

Try your own or use my template:

*May this water _____.
As I cleanse my body, _____.
When I step out, I will be _____, full of _____.*

ENGAGING WITH SPIRITS AND ENERGIES
IN A SHARED SPACE

If you live in a city, there's a good chance you rent your space, which means your
space was also someone else's home before—and that it will be again. More than
that, cities themselves (especially older ones) have developed and changed so
much that there is often a residue—whether energetically or culturally—that,
well, *lingers.*

The transient energy of city life makes for an interesting living space; your
neighbors may come and go. New buildings may be built alongside your own.
You may never know who lived in your space before you. And even if you own
your home, someone likely lived in it before you did.

Whether or not you believe in conscious ghosts, spirits, energetic residue, or
memory matter—whatever you choose to call it—the idea of being "haunted" is

pervasive through cultures and time. Our subconscious minds pick up on things we often do not, which is the reason we may feel a certain way in a space but not know why. Sure, it could be a house "looks" creepy but is as innocuous as a newborn kitten, or it could be carbon monoxide (which is known to cause feelings of dread or paranoia). But let's be honest—that can't account for every ghastly experience.

If you sense you may be sharing your space with something *else*—and that *elseness* doesn't seem harmful—you may want to perform the following apartment haunting ritual, not only for peace of mind, but also to acknowledge the elephant in the room. You will also want to state you have a boundary and you wish it not to be crossed. Your space is yours—although if you do believe in ghosts, it can't hurt to contact an experienced medium.

The below practice comes recommended by a psychic who told me my current apartment is haunted, but also from cultures that embrace death. In New Orleans, one restaurant leaves a table set for the spirits of the place, and although this may partially be for the amusement of tourists, it is based in practices to appease and live alongside spirits.

I use the practice to work with energies that seem "stuck" in my space. It needn't solely be a ghost (with an identity); it can be done after an argument, or if you've had some people over with bad energy. It can also be used to acknowledge the memory of the space.

- Write a letter to the ghost, spirit, or energy. Let it know you'd like your space and you're asking it to not linger. On the other hand, if you want to acknowledge something that happened in your space, say so. Sometimes just acknowledging what is there makes it go away and sometimes acknowledging it makes *you* feel more autonomous, less like ducking through its shadows.
....
- Set the letter out on a clean table along with a glass of wine or tea. Offer the drink to your spirit. Perhaps you want to leave out some bread for them as well. Light a candle and shut off the lights.
....

- Sitting in the space, read the letter aloud, and then listen. Notice the energy. Notice the temperature. Notice any feelings, intuitions, visions, physical sensations, or emotions that arise.

Afterward, it's a smart idea to cleanse the space in a way that feels right to you, like with smoking protective herbs or with your moon water spray. Make sure you move through each room and speak your intent to cleanse, protect, and purify the space aloud. No matter your belief systems, the very act of declaring your intent aloud carries the ability to shift reality. What you speak is a spell.

CLEANSING YOUR SPACE: MOON WATER MAGIC

Moon water is one of the most wonderful ways of creating magic easily or on-the-go while traveling, for example, and it's available to all of us. Cultures and traditions across the world have turned to the moon for her magic. From the ancient Greeks to Indigenous Americans, moon lore, deities, and magic have always lit the way, for the moon holds power over the seasons, nature, and our bodies.

Moon water is water charged under the moon's light (or with its energy), to be used as part of spell work, as a cleanser, as part of your beauty routine, or as a way to shift the stale energy in a space. The moon, of course, offers us

MOONLIT APARTMENT MAGIC

NEW MOON Set goals for apartment updates; make a list of plants you'd like to buy or ingredients for kitchen magic. This is also a time to show gratitude, enjoy, and reflect on your space and its energies. This is also a great time to do a space cleansing or to commit to a new household routine, like avoiding dish buildup or a morning tidying before work. It could also be a good time to research your apartment's history or tune into the energies.

....

WAXING MOON As the moon grows bigger, this is the time to reorganize and take action. Bring plants into your home, and empower your space so what you need is accessible to you. This is also a great time to design or redo a mini altar space.

....

FULL MOON Get creative with your space. Use color magic by pulling some fresh flowers, reorganizing books according to their colors, hanging up more art, making art for yourself, or rearranging furniture for maximum beauty and comfort. The moon's energy is at its fullest, so cast a spell for household peace or creative energy. Light a single candle on your windowsill and let its fiery energy power up your space.

....

WANING MOON Now's *the time* to start releasing that which you do not need. Declutter in a way that works for you! A decluttered space allows for mental clarity, and cleansing can heal a space. If you are a maximalist, that's okay—but do not be afraid to let go of that which doesn't serve you. This is also a time to make a nice dinner for yourself, sit with a glass of wine or tea, and quietly tune into the city sounds outside your window or the energy within your space.

its duality (its power of luminosity *and* its shadowy energies). It offers us the power of transformation as its cycles dictate nature.

It is a wise idea to have moon water on hand or make it often—especially on full or new moons when the energy is intense or when you want to power up a spell for new projects, respectively. Place water in a mason jar on a window-sill (or anywhere you can catch the moon's light). But what if you can't see the moon or if your window looks out onto another building?

There is a solution to this problem. No, it doesn't ask you to go on some elaborate witchy quest for spots to hide your mason jar (which sounds rather fun, if not a bit risky).

Rather, it requires reframing and a bow to the power of the deep moon whose energy we can *always* feel even without seeing it. Scorpio moon? You don't need to be standing outside in the starlit sky to feel those lusty, intense vibes. The same goes for moon water.

Sidney Eileen, an animistic, polytheist witch beautifully examined this issue of indirect moonlight for Patheos Pagan's the Agora blog:

> The energies of the moon are pervasive, if more subtle in the shadows, and sometimes the energy of subtlety is advantageous. It reminds us that even when we can't see the light, can't see a way forward, such things still exist and affect us. All we need to do is pay attention and hold the knowledge of them in our hearts.[1]

You can collect the water come morning and funnel it into a spray bottle or keep it in a lidded mason jar. Below are easy, accessible ways of using it:

- Mix it with your moisturizers for a dose of power
- Anoint scrolls of paper written with your incantations and wishes

---

1 Sidney Eileen, "The Balancing Path: Moon Water with No Moonlight," Patheos Pagan—The Agora Blog, accessed January 18, 2021, https://tinyurl.com/eileenmoonwater.

- Make a house cleanser with it to energetically cleanse and power up your space
- Spritz it before performing a ritual
- Drink it to be imbued with the moon's magic and potency
- Make moon water in a new space or hotel room with which to cleanse and purify the space

ANOTHER IDEA: Write poetry of the moon; capture its liminal essence in a poem. What does her magnetic pull make you feel? What energy do you sense during certain phases? Write a moon-inspired poem per cycle, just to see how your voice and its energy shifts. Poetry is a way of prayer, for poems are a devotional act to the moon.

A NOTE ON MOON MAGIC AND CRYSTALS: You can also charge your crystals by the light of the moon (and yes, they will still be charged without direct moonlight). Magic makers love to charge their crystals with moonlight to empower them and to cleanse them of all older, stagnant energies they collect after being handled or laid out. Once powered up, you can arrange them in your space to inspire you and infuse it with magic—and you can carry them with you if you want to benefit from their energies. You don't have to believe a crystal has an innate energy to work with it, although many people do.

A crystal can also serve as a symbol (you pick what it symbolizes to you; for example, I carry a rose quartz when I travel to remind me that softness and love follow me wherever I go). Crystals are also a great tool for grounding if you need something to hold in a moment of crowded-train panic or anxiety.

MAKING MAGIC IN THE KITCHEN

Mary-Grace Fahrun, author of *Italian Folk Magic: Rue's Kitchen Witchery,* says she bases her practice around her kitchen—a space she keeps extremely tidy and organized because it is sacred. It is a space where all of the elements come together and where intentional actions take place.

In kitchens, we can brew coffee when we need a boost (an underrated water ritual!) or whisper a spell over a bubbling pot (who actually has a cauldron?) of stew or while sprinkling herbs into a slow cooker (a great idea for if you have to leave the house; the spell continues without you). It is a space where friends gather to share wine and sorrows. It is a space where roommates deepen their bonds. It's where tea is made for the sick. It's where we hydrate when we are anxious and exhausted. It's where we experience the pleasures of being alive. It's where we connect with foods that speak to our ancestry, to the seasons, and to the city we live in. It's a space where the magic exists in spades—there is fire, there is water, and there are herbs. The simple acts of making, enjoying, and tidying are all ritualistic in nature. In any preparation or cooking, imbue the act with intention and a visualization of outcome.

"It is my temple, shrine, and altar," Fahrun writes. In most city living situations, kitchens are small or shared—but that makes them no less magical. Here are some ways you can embrace kitchen witchery and the sacredness of your own space.

- **Get yourself a good pot**. You'll want one that is *yours*, that is large, and that you can use as a cauldron (i.e., the pot you turn to repeatedly to cook meals with intention). As Fahrun says, the cookware we return to time and again will always yield a delicious meal and it will cast your spells. While it's easy to use what's around, or use your roommates' pots, this is one item you'll want to have for life.

- **Whisper intentions over your food.** This is a sort of alchemy. You are changing it from "just food" into magic. Bless your food so that whomever eats it is blessed. Use words that feel intuitive to you. A simple, "I thank this basil for its beauty and flavor. May it bless this meal and whomever enjoys it" can work. It can be even simpler than that by whispering "thank you," to the food you are preparing. Don't be afraid to hold food in your hands to energize it before throwing it into the pot. Don't be afraid to write words of magic—"healing," "harmony," "inspiration"—into boiling water with the end of your wooden spoon.

- **Keep your kitchen tidy, especially if you are into kitchen witchery.** Sweep it in the daytime to catch any dust or particles, and sprinkle bits of salt in its corners to protect the space. The energy of a kitchen dictates the energy of a home. If it is clean and clear, you are clearer mentally, and you are ready to brew a healing pot of tea or make a magical meal anytime without the cluttered energy of dishes and spills. If you can't physically clean the kitchen all the time, just clear a portion of counter space and prep your tea or food there.

- **Tea is magic.** Even if you're no chef (like me), imbibing tea and coffee are easy ritual acts. They are ways we take a breath, to hydrate, to energize, to find relief, and to offer support. Experiment with ways of brewing tea and coffee that feel right to you; perhaps you like a pour-over because the act of pouring the water into the grinds while saying a few words of intention for

COMMON HERBS THAT DOUBLE
AS MAGIC INGREDIENTS

Anything is magic, of course. Your oat milk is magic if you pour it with intention. But there are some herbs that are beloved by witches and herbalists alike for their magical properties (as well as their taste). You can smoke cleanse with certain herbs, crush herbs and spices for teas, place them in bundles or sachets to hang over your bed or doorway, or sprinkle them into bathwater (see **Resources, pp. 141, for books on herbal magic**).

Basil
Purification, love, magic,
and protection

Rosemary
Protection against negative energy,
healing, vitality

Black Pepper
Ward against negativity,
confidence booster,
limiting thoughts remover

Parsley
Protection, love,
connection to the dead

Bay Leaves
*Success, money, magic,
achievement*

Red Pepper
*Blockage and unwanted
energy remover*

Chili Pepper
Protection from the evil eye

Cinnamon
*Invigoration, warmth, abundance,
passion, and love*

Thyme
*Courage, protection,
and purification*

Salt
Protection

your day is comforting. Perhaps you like to boil your water in a pot and watch the water shake and rattle as it boils, infusing your tea with energy and power. Try this: In the middle of the day—on a weekend or weekday if you're home—stand quietly in your kitchen after it's been cleaned. Feel its calmness. Feel its energy. Feel it's a space for you to create and heal and nourish. Sip a cup of tea and find gratitude for the moment.

....

• **Create ancestral foods.** The holy space of the kitchen allows you to con-nect—through food, spices, and the very process of making—with your ances-tral self and the deeply embedded cultural sparks that light you up today. This is a bloodline practice or a chosen family practice. Learn the recipes from continents and countries and regions. Make the food while meditating on lineage and all you carry, all you preserve, and all you will let go. Call on your ancestors (those you know, and those you don't) to be there with you, to bless your food, and to offer you wisdom. Be mindful as you eat; it isn't just a meal. It's a physical rite of connection. On weekends, I like to make bruschetta or gambas al ajillo or Olivier salad — a sort of ancestral ritual.

....

- **Tap into the culinary history of your city.** By exploring the taste of your local land, you are collaborating with its energy—asking it to nourish you, protect you, and be a source of power. What are your regional or local dishes, and how were they inspired? What are some herbs native to your region? If you can visit a farmers market (often, people come from more rural regions into the city on weekends and set up shop in central locations), see if you can get your hands on the local honey (which can help boost immune function) or wine (which is just delicious).

- **Keep a magical object hanging in your kitchen.** This may be a symbol of good luck (like a horseshoe or milagros), or it can be a symbol of protection (like the hamsa or cimaruta, which ward away the evil eye). You can also keep a candle for use only when cooking intentionally, or you may choose to keep fresh flowers on the countertop. The idea is to acknowledge and create a sacred space that reminds you of its—and your—power.

- **Clear the air.** Open your windows after you cook and enjoy your meal to reset the energy.

- **Raise plants.** If you happen to have a kitchen window for light, having a few potted plants—that you grew yourself—is an incredibly potent way to enjoy food and worship nature. Basil, rosemary, parsley, mint, oregano, cilantro, and arugula are some common favorites that are generally very fuss-free (but do require bright light and may take time). Each time you take a pinch, thank the plant and throw it into your food with a word of blessing. You can even get cat grass, which is nutritious, super easy to grow, and can be fed to your furry friend (so they can experience the magic too!). There are plenty of delivery services for these plants, but a pack of seeds, some soil, and a potter shouldn't cost you much. Some people also opt for a small incubator, which does a lot of the work.

- **Grind your herbs.** Keep a mortar and pestle on hand—a sturdy wooden one is usually great—to grind herbs. The act of physically grinding your herbs is a kitchen alchemy that can be meditative and powerful. Don't worry, though, you can also symbolically perform this kitchen alchemy with preground herbs.

- **Write down your recipes.** Include the incantations you use. You may start to notice when you make ancestral meals or use certain phrases while cooking, things happen.

- **Eat in season.** In some cities, it's harder to find a farmers market or local greens, especially in the winter when open-air markets are closed. Sometimes, the farmers markets that do exist are out of the way or too pricy. You can still eat in season with the basics. Depending on where you live, those basics will change change. In the United States, you can eat seasonally with easy-to-find foods. Even if they're not local, they're in cycle with nature. Summer is a great time for bananas, lemons, apples, summer squash, mangos, okra, and peaches. Autumn is a time for spinach, pomegranates, pumpkins, cauliflower, peas, and mushrooms. Winter offers sweet potatoes, beets, yams, and collard greens. Spring brings rhubarb, strawberries, cabbage, and celery. There are also many overlapping foods through the seasons! Other options: Check out local farm-to-table delivery services or grow your own foods. Easy-to-grow foods (which do require a windowsill with light, some soil, a pot, and a willingness to try) include limes, lemons, avocados, tomatoes, green beans, carrots, and strawberries.

THE PORTABLE ALTAR &
THE MAGICAL MEDICINE CABINET

Back to accessibility. There's this notion that for magic to "work," it must be aesthetically pleasing and Instagrammable, expensive, or complicated. There's this idea that things create an aha moment, when the aha moment is really in the deep quiet of the process. It is when we believe our words and speak them. It is when we visualize with our whole hearts.

Magic only works if you do. It is the belief, the prayer, the intent, the deep truth that magic is hungry for. It is the simple words uttered into the rain. It is the hands clasped before sleep. It is the rawness of being human that gives it its power.

The tools, actions, sounds, and aesthetics of ritual certainly augment it, offering us a way of directing energy and relaying intent. Actions are potent. Things carry energy. But we are magic beings, and we mustn't let magic become ableist in nature. There are things in this book I cannot do on bad days, but in the end, we can still all embrace sacredness by breathing, speaking, or visualizing. So altar or no altar, you are magical enough.

Now, as someone living with chronic illness, I find days in bed are no longer rare. My chronic fatigue has ramped up in the past three or four years, and slipped in like the coming winter chill—almost without me noticing until it was something I had to be mindful about. So many of my magic-making friends live with a chronic disease or condition of some sort, something that makes it hard to have the energy for elaborate setups. In cities, chronic illnesses may be worsened by things like demanding traffic, high flights of stairs, and noise and light pollution (overstimulation, anyone?).

Should I still want material objects of sacredness, a shoebox (or lidded box, jewelry box, woven basket or bowl, glass tray, or small ottoman) will make a fine altar. I've even seen someone online (thanks, @tiredqueer via

Amino Apps!) mention they'd even used an Altoid box! I recommend keeping an in-bed altar; these tiny altars can infuse your day with magic while you recoup from a tough week, lie in bed with a flare-up, or just want some downtime.

Mine is a beautiful cardboard lidded box from the perfume maker Officina Profumo-Farmaceutica di Santa Maria Novella. Within, I keep a few shells, a small incense cone, perfume I got on a trip, a few crystals, a notepad, an oil from a Brooklyn occult shop called Catland, a tiny deck of tarot cards, and a lighter with a few votives. It is simple and beautiful and right at arm's reach.

NOTE: This portable altar is probably one you could even travel with!

The medicine cabinet altar is an alternative that may suit those of you who want to condense your space (and make your morning more meaningful and glamorous). A single shelf or two can be devoted to apothecary jars, elixirs, creams (whose containers are decorated with sigils, of course!), a crystal or two for morning meditation, essential oils, programmed lipstick or shaving cream, perfumes, a tiny candle to be lit while getting ready, and anything else you see fit.

Below are some questions to get you thinking about your altar setup. These are not meant to be answered all at once, nor will they all have an answer. Rather, they're to get you thinking.

- What items are important to you that seem mundane but are actually meaningful, and how may they be incorporated into your altar?
- What colors, textures, items, or energies are an expression of who you are and how you envision your altar looking?
- What sort of "fancy" witchy items can be swapped out with household items?
- Would it be a temporary, permanent, portable, or miniature altar?
- Where would you place it. Should it be private, or can it be out in the open?
- If you create an altar, will it be a general altar for all of your magical workings, or will it be an altar dedicated to a hobby, craft, life goal, or passion. What may be laid upon it?
- Would you update your altar seasonally?
- Would you dedicate your altar to a god, spirit, archetype, or deity?
- How can you honor and celebrate your city or city spirit on the altar?
- Do you have a schedule intended for altar updating? Would you tend to it during each full moon or with each new astrological season, for example?
- What would be kept inside a portable, stay-in-bed altar?
- Do you have any ancestral, cultural, or personal practices that inspire the altar?
- If you are moving into a new apartment and want to erect an altar right away, what are the most important things to have on hand? What makes you feel safe, stable, and at home?
- What would be inside your travel altar?
- How will you bless your altar? Will you surround it in salt, or cleanse it with smoke? Will you purify its items by moonlight or with a cleansing crystal like selenite?

ENCHANT

EMBRACING THE CITY'S
LIGHT AND SHADOW

HAVE YOU EVER WALKED THROUGH your city at night, with its golden, warm light drenching the street, only to find yourself in one of those ecstatic "city moments?" Its energy and your energy align; the external and your internal world collapse into one. Everything feels warm, fuzzy, and connected; you know the feeling. That's a certain city magic. The overhead train may be soaring over you, or you may be emerging from the underground into the din of voices—and yet, it all feels right, chosen, asked-for, appreciated.

These moments happen often for me when I cross the Brooklyn Bridge; to my left is the Statue of Liberty (her light symbolizing all that I believe—that people should be free, and we should help our fellow humankind). To my right are all the buildings that etch the fabric of my personal journey. New York City was the place where I discovered and created myself.

But let's not glamorize it all. There are so many moments of doubt, financial insecurity, and exhaustion. And there's the well of sociopolitical issues we see hyperexaggerated in the cityscape: gentrification, massive wealth gaps, racism. The list goes on.

But to find the embers in our cities, we must also know its shadows and its liminal spaces. We must be willing to straddle the thresholds, to find the spots that resonate, vibrate, and illuminate. We must be willing to look into crevices, to feel the pulses, and to hear the silences.

EMBRACING LEY LINES, CROSSROADS, LIMINAL SPACES, AND THE CITY CENTER

Cities, as you know by now, are full of energy—the energy of the ancient earth, people, and power structures. Consider the concept of ley lines (which go by many names), areas of intense energy; these have, in some way, been embraced by cultures ancient and modern, although not everyone agrees on what they are or how they are formed.

Ley lines are essentially spaces where powerful energy currents occur. Many people believe they are found at sacred spots of power (think of Stonehenge or the Giza Pyramid Complex). They are also found in spaces where, say, water meets the earth. In urban environments, the general theory is ley lines occur where foot traffic is high and where power complexes stand. The ley line discussion is complex, and it's worth looking into the ley line history of your city.

There are often points of power carved by Indigenous communities that you'll want to know about. One way people seek this energy is by using dowsing rods or pendulums (a basic Google search ought to tell you where ley lines are near you), or by intuiting energy shifts in certain places.

A walk through your city may yield some interesting energetic patterns. How does the energy shift in places like cemeteries, rivers, governmental buildings, shrines, burial grounds, haunted spots, ancient natural spaces (like natural rock cave formations in public parks), fountains where crowds gather, obelisks, memorials, or liminal spaces like natural trails leading into and out of the city?

City energy, whether ancient or manmade, is ripe, and we can harness it. Stand in these spaces and feel the energy rooting through the earth and into you. Use it to power your intentions and visualizations; you can silently work with this energy in person simply by focusing.

Crossroads and Liminal Spaces

Everyone I know jokes about city witchery: "It's not like you can just go out to the crossroads to work your spell." I've heard it many times now. I suppose it's rather true; a crossroad in a city is usually hard to get to by foot, or a recipe for an accident.

These liminal spaces—the "betwixt and between"—are potent, and witches know this. They are considered the convergence of space, time, energy, the natural world, the living world, and the otherworld. It is perfectly fine to wish you could tune into the energy of a crossroad, or burn or dispose of a spell or letter at the crossroads to ritualize your intention. Luckily, we can tap into the energy of crossroads without having access to them in an urban environment!

The liminal is something humans understand innately, even if we don't explicitly think about it. We've all been told the tale of *Cinderella*: What happens at midnight, that liminal hour? Something transforms, of course. A shift occurs. A spell is broken. What happens when we fly? Time goes on hold. We *feel* we are neither here nor there.

Other liminalities: spiritual limbo, a space before the afterlife. The space between asleep and awake. The special energy of the golden hour, when light makes way for night. The liminal is something we humans need. Perhaps it's a way for us to live out the many selves we contain, and the spaces between our conscious and subconscious states. It is how we reconcile and engage our natural darkness.

We can access the liminal during meditation (visualizing crossroads or layers of time, if your spell requires it, can be helpful):

- Conducting a spell just at the moment sunset begins is yet another way of bringing the crossroads to you.

- Taking a walk through the city at dusk or standing in a doorway while reciting an incantation can help you tune in the city's liminal frequencies.

- Writing a poem is a way of tuning into liminal ideas; a poem holds space for language to be two things at once—sad *and* joyful, dark *and* light.

- Call on the liminal deities of thresholds (and the psychopomps, who deliver the dead over the "border" to the afterlife) during spells and rituals to help us tap into the energy of crossroads.

But what about the lack of crossroads for disposing magical items? My suggestion: Burn it (in a bowl near your sink), bury it (even at the bottom of a potted plant!), flush it, or throw it in the trash— all in a ritual manner. If you want something off your property, a garbage can near a graveyard is a great option. Just be ethical and don't litter.

Seeking Energy in the City's Center

Every city has a technical, *geographical* city center. In fact, in Paris, tourists and locals alike flock to "kilometre zero," just outside of the Notre Dame Cathedral (now under reconstruction due to the fire it suffered in 2019), where a brass plate marks the very center of the city. People have come to kiss, dance, and leave coins at this spot—and to feel its energy.

In your city's point zero—which may be a place you've visited or not at all—you may want to stand and feel its resonance, the energy of its structure, history, and people surrounding you.

Where is your city's geographical center? Google ought to be able to tell you where it is and if it's accessible (sometimes it's in water or somewhere you just don't want to go). You can find somewhere close to it and soak up its nearby energy if it's safe and practical. This may be a good time to journal, meditate, or do some grounding work.

Cemetery Magic: Working with the City's Dead

You can learn a lot about a city by looking at how it treats its dead, and how beloved its cemeteries may be. For one, a cemetery is a shared space between the living, the dead, and the society at large. A cemetery or a graveyard (which

is attached to a churchyard, although most people use them synonymously) often function as one of the only representations of how society publicly or openly faces grief and acknowledges death (in the West, we like to tidy it away and pretend it doesn't really happen). So, aside from it housing our dead, cemeteries are very tangible and visible representations of the life cycle and the sacredness we all inherently desire to connect with, even if we don't live in a very death-positive society.

Some cities are cemetery cities, or cities of the dead. I think of New Orleans's famous St. Louis Cemetery No. 1; everyone wants to visit it, learn about its burial practices, and leave fresh flowers for its dead, especially Voodoo Queen Marie Laveau. In Brooklyn's Green-Wood Cemetery (which helped inspire the concept of green spaces and public parks in the city), musical events, tours, and death parlors are held; there is a sense in both of these places that death is most certainly not a bad or macabre word; rather these resting places are an extension of who we are, were, and will be.

Cemetery magic can help us get in touch with the heart of our city—for when a soul is buried in a place, it is, in a sense, there forever. Some believe a soul buried in a particular location watches over its city; some people work with the spirits of artists, poets, musicians, and other beloved figures who lived, loved, and worked in a city.

CITY WITCHERY

A stroll through a cemetery—being mindful of whose graves are there, and if you would like to pay respects to them in some way—is an easy way to connect with the cyclical nature of existence and to confront death. It is a way of experiencing a place of liminality and meditating on that distinct still, shushed energy. It is also a beautiful way to experience nature in a city if the cemetery is maintained and respected by its living community. If it's not, then that's something worth noting and reflecting on.

Picnicking in a cemetery is a way to honor death, time, a specific departed person, and your own experience of being alive. I've always found it as a way of experiencing the pleasures of being alive—wine, food, water—while sitting upon a threshold. Offering a bit to the dead is a common way of paying respect.

Cemeteries are also amazing places to forage for altar items, such as pine cones, dirt, leaves, flowers, or stones. Be sure to ask permission first and pay attention to what surfaces when you do ask if you can take something. Bringing cemetery items into your altar or home space can help with banishing or binding rituals, or to necromancy practices.

Cemetery visits are also opportunities to call upon liminal entities or archetypes, to heal through the sheer expression of grief, and to work with oracle or tarot cards. In a cemetery, there is a special energy that removes the barriers between this and the otherworld, and it is palpable.

For city witches who work with the spirits, energies, or archetypes of place, the cemetery can help you feel connected to the deep history of place, especially that which requires reckoning and acknowledgment. I recommend visiting the entire cemetery, even spaces where unmarked graves exist; they are often the graves of the poor or people who have been sadly forgotten by time.

NOTE: If you are interested in a particular grave, or the history of a specific cemetery or graveyard, you can always work with the cemetery, holy building, or local historical society to find out more about a particular grave (you'd be surprised at the customs and stories cemeteries offer).

SHADOW WORKING YOUR CITY

"Ant swarming City
City full of dreams
Where in broad day the specter tugs your sleeve."

—CHARLES BAUDELAIRE

A city's heart is made of many opposing valves. The blood of violence, poverty, and loneliness pumps alongside the magic of community, art, and opportunity. Trust funds share space with searing debt. Advocacy shares space with greed. And where there is a great park drenched in sunlight, there is always a predator lurking in the shadows. Every city has its Jekylls and its Hydes, and at times these entities and energies seem to climb up through our fire escapes and settle deep into our bones.

If humans have shadow selves—which are as Erich Neumann puts it, a collection of "qualities, capacities and tendencies which do not harmonize with the collective values. . .that dark region of the personality which is unknown and unrecognized by the ego,"—do cities not have them as well?

Consider *Mulholland Drive*'s "Dumpster monster" scene. On a sunny day in Los Angeles, there's this horrifying, seemingly surreal monster-being that appears from behind a Dumpster; the scene is filled with dread and anxiety, and the sense that everything seemingly normal has an underbelly. That's the shadow self, the shit that lurks, the stuff people try to deny or hide away. The key to that scene was the character chose to see it. He peered behind and expected it.

Shadow working our cities—or any city—is a radical act. It's a commitment to truth and a way to hold a mirror up to ourselves. How does our city bring out the monster in us? How are we upholding ideas or behaviors or beliefs that strain the city? How are we contributing to the demise of a neighborhood? Or, how are we creating good? What have we placed upon the altar of our cities?

The beauty of a city is it functions as a dream (albeit depending on to whom and in what context), a tabula rasa, a spell in the works. People are born here, flock here, struggle here, achieve here—everyone's story is different. And so, a city is a glamorous idea, but it's also more than that. It is what it *is* and what it does to its people. Shadow work allows us to see the city for what it gives us, for what we give it, *and* for what it is, as if we didn't exist.

New Orleans, for example, is many things. It is second line bands marching through the streets, carousel bars, ghost stories, and beignets at midnight. But it is also a place that fell into the depths and had to crawl its way out many times. There is death and high poverty, and the way tourism affects locals and culture.

As Carl Jung says, "How can I be substantial if I do not cast a shadow? I must have a dark side also if I am to be whole."

How can we acknowledge all of a space's aspects? We must keep an eye on the dark and the quiet—for beneath the glitter, there are catacombs. The witch is one who notices.

Shadow working your city may include:

- **Constructing an altar dedicated to your city.** Perhaps it's an altar in memory of those who were lost, or perhaps it's an altar that you light for the city's

sick and most vulnerable. Maybe it's an altar dedicated to an archetype or entity that presides over the city and to whom you call on for guidance and protection during crisis. This can be especially effective if you feel limited and distraught. You can erect on a specific day—such as a city anniversary—or whenever you feel compelled. Spend time with the altar and do not stray from it. This is a good idea for anyone getting used to life in a new city as well.

- **Writing a poem about the chthonic underbelly of your city—its sinister secrets, out-in-the-open wounds, dark dates, and tragedies.** Charles Baudelaire's famous poetic work, *The Flowers of Evil,* looks at the industrialization of Paris, the demolition of medieval spaces that held profound history, the bourgeois, and the feelings of isolation and disconnection to one's own city. It's a tremendous read for any city witch or traveler to Paris. In fact, the poet believed it was gravely important that artists capture the essence of the metropolis.

  Now is your chance to write a poem that speaks to the shadows in your city. Recite the poem into an open space, such as a public park or cemetery.

CITY WITCHERY

This communication with city energy can help us have a deeper connection to where we live and how we experience city life. It can be extremely hard to experience the beauty of a city *knowing* how much suffering there is or was in it. Do not look away. If you feel a need to visit sites where traumatic events took place, bring a flower or a token of respect with you if possible. Be sure to protect your energy in these spaces.

....

- **Understanding how literal shadows affect space.** In the article, "Mapping the Shadows of New York City," authors Quoctrung Bui and Jeremy White write the financial district in Manhattan is one of the shadowiest spaces in the city—literally: "Developers here built the city's first skyscrapers on plots originally intended for Dutch villagers. The result is a maze of dark narrow corridors formed by tall street walls that block out much of the sky."[2] Not surprising that such a money-hungry space is so dark, huh? The world is funny like that.

  Seek out your city's or neighborhood's literal shadows and notice where your city or your apartment gets the most light. Are there neighborhoods built under railway tracks? Are there skyscrapers blocking light? Is your apartment built in between two taller buildings, plunging your space into darkness? How does light affect space? How does a lack of light affect your bedroom, your mood, your magic, and your connection to the city? Take note where shadows fall and what creates them. Take note of how space and energies shift in gray dim light. Also, take note of how a neighborhood finds resiliency and power in its shadow.

  If lack of literal light affects your own magic, find ways to seek it and find ways to create light where it doesn't exist: Candles, early-morning walks, sunlamps, color magic (bright colors especially) are all helpful. Notice, too,

---

2 Quoctrung Bui and Jeremy White, "Mapping the Shadows of New York City: Every Building, Every Block," New York Times, accessed January 18, 2021, https://tinyurl.com/nyshadows.

if you work better in the shadows, and how dimness and darkness inspire, affect, or hurt you.

How do shadow spaces represent the things we deny, look away from, or erase from our cities' narratives?

THE HELM OF DARKNESS AND THE EXPOSED SELF

"In great cities . . . walking, witnessing, being in public, are as much part of the design and purpose as is being inside to eat, sleep, make shoes or love or music."

—**REBECCA SOLNIT**, *Wanderlust: A History of Walking*

Ah, to gaze and not be gazed upon in return! Cities afford us a helm of darkness, that which in Greek mythology is known as the Cap of Hades—for it obscures one from view. When Hades wore it, he could become one with the shadows and move freely into the underworld.

There is magic in being surrounded by people while being invisible. Of course this invisibility varies city to city, but when we wear our helm, we learn to observe, to move through shadows, and to be out-of-focus. When you are alone in the city, envision a protective shield around you body that becomes opaque, blurring you from view. Remove all distractions (headphones, books, etc.) and see how the shield shifts, moves, and breaths. Sit in a bar and observe. Sit in a café and listen. Be mindful about *just being* so you can be receptive.

If you quietly ask for wisdom, messages, and/or signs from the city, you will get them—but you have to listen. Great spaces to be invisible are parks, crowded wine bars, poetry readings, bookshops, street markets, and spaces and landmarks with lots of foot traffic—think Chicago's The Bean or Mexico City's Castillo de Chapultepec.

The best part? Everywhere you go, you will observe how a space's or attraction's particular energy affects *the collective energy* as well as your own. This

practice is incredible for establishing a deeper link to your intuition and for being able to better connect with others.

At the other end of the spectrum, invisibility becomes exposure.

I've always been enamored with Edward Hopper's paintings of city land-scapes, like *Night Windows, Office in a Small City, Morning in a City*. If you haven't seen them, I encourage you to pull them up on Google. The works offer a quiet, eerie glimpse into city life: people gazing out of buildings, the looming city always staring back. People doing intimate things (like drinking coffee) under the watchful eye of the City. We are always on the verge of or being watched. Viewed. Found.

As you move through the city, decide you want to be seen. Perhaps this is a chance to dissolve your shield and notice what changes. Do people ask you for directions? Do you stumble upon a chatty bartender?

If Hopper's paintings also make you feel just a tad uneasy, it's because the city is a strange creature. We know we are always on display, and yet we are hidden in plain sight. We move through this dichotomy with ease, mostly, although it can be unsettling. This liminality is a gift and a curse, and must be understood to be balanced.

A MOVING RITUAL:
FOR THOSE COMING AND THOSE LEAVING

"Love in its fullest form is a series of deaths and rebirths. . . . To love means to embrace and at the same time to withstand many endings, and many, many beginnings—all in the same relationship."

—CLARISSA PINKOLA ESTÉS, *Women Who Run with the Wolves: Myths and Stories of the Wild Woman Archetype*

More people in cities are renters than homeowners, so it's normal for people to move yearly or every few years. This means any space—your bedroom, your very bed, your sense of home—will change, will be reoriented, and will be updated. You, too, will be changed and reoriented.

They say moving is one of the most stressful things, but it's not just because packing and unpacking is terrible (and it is). It's because each new home requires a different anchor, and in the interim, we are anchorless.

On the night before you leave—or when you can find some quiet, peaceful time to focus, you'll need:
- A candle
- Scissors and a piece of paper
- A broom
- Salt

First, do a final, intentional sweep your space—especially where you sleep or spent most of your time. Sweep from the outside in, envisioning closure and goodbye. This is a gesture that says, "I am gathering my energies and I am receptive to moving on." In some folk magic traditions, salt is thrown into corners—and then swept inward—to purify the space as well. Collect the dust in a specific bag and dispose of it in a trash bin *outside* the home.

After your place is swept, light a single candle to say goodbye to the past and to illuminate the start of your new journey. Moving can be emotional—due to a toxic environment, a breakup, or just raised rent. It can also be exciting and a fresh start. It's okay to feel all of these things, and it's a transition and occasion worth ritualizing either way.

On a piece of paper, draw a line down the middle. On the left, write out a few memories or qualities of the space and city you're leaving (especially if you are moving to a new city). On the right, list your goals, plans, hopes, and what you intend to bring with you to the experience. Aloud, ask the new space or city to be welcoming and gentle.

Be mindful, you are saying goodbye (even to the good!) and manifesting positivity for the future (even if it's hard). Use the scissors to cut the paper in half. You can burn the left side and keep the right.

When you arrive in your new apartment, cleanse the apartment literally and magically. Bury the paper with your future plans and goals in a potted plant, or place it on your altar. Let it bloom.

RESTORE

SELF-CARE RITUALS AND TIPS
FOR THE OVERSATURATED,
OVERWORKED, EXHAUSTED,
AND MAGIC-LACKING CITY WITCH

THERE'S NO POINT IN WRITING a book of city magic that denies the muck and chaos of this life. Each city has its own unique limitations and pain points (looking at you, subway delays, overcrowding, financial barriers, and constant construction). COVID-19 has no doubt changed our cities deeply as well.

City magic isn't about denying the hardships of city life; it's about embracing and contributing to the good—and choosing to work within the complexities and the shadows. One of the most common conversations I have with friends—and perhaps you do too—is our nuanced feelings around city life. A city is a beast. It is hungry. It is a machine. But it is also a sun. It is a guide. It is a poem.

Below are some accessible tips, tricks, rituals, and practices to help you cope on those days when you feel like packing up and getting out, moving to the middle nowhere.

The good news? There is magic all around you; you just have to notice it. As Mya Spalter writes in *Enchantments: A Modern Witch's Guide to Self-Possession*, "That's what witches do: We look for magic, for divinity, in everything. What's more, we allow ourselves to find it, even in the seemingly mundane."

- **Teas for the tired:** Reach for teas with chamomile, lavender, valerian, and ashwagandha on days when you've hit max output. Take a cup of tea and sit quietly, focusing only the sensation and flavor of the tea.

- **Herbs for revitalization.** According to *The Herbal Alchemist's Handbook: A Complete Guide to Magickal Herbs and How to Use Them* by Karen Harrison, colorful and bright solar herbs—like angelica, calendula, chamomile, St. John's Wort, juniper, rosemary, saffron, and frankincense are  excellent for restoring equilibrium, health, vitality, and energy—especially when rundown. To reap the benefits, you can imbibe these herbs via pre-made tea or herbal infusion (one teaspoon of herb plus sixteen ounces of water). Better yet? Let the infusion sit out in the sunlight to power up.

- **Ritual bathing.** I've been indulging in a ritual bath straight out of the pages of Cyndi Brannen's *Entering Hekate's Garden: The Magick, Medicine & Mystery of Plant Spirit Witchcraft*. It calls for one tablespoon on yarrow plus one tablespoon of mugwort (which you can get at an apothecary or an online shop; see **Resources**) placed into a cup of boiling water. When it cools, pour it into your bathtub and step in. If you can't get your hands on herbs, (see **Washroom Magic pp. 82**), charge some epsom salt or bubble bath with healing energy. Take a bath and let the water cleanse your body of all frenetic, sad, and overworked energies.

- **Pull a tarot card in the middle of a busy day, asking the deck to reveal insight as to how you may trudge forward.** Meditate on its message and find a way to apply its insight immediately. Sometimes, we need a little help from the great mystery to help us find a way. The break will also be restorative.

- **Program an anxiety relief crystal.** Choose one with a color that softens and cradles you, and one that is big enough to hold and roll over your palm but small enough to be secretive. If you are stuck on a crowded subway car or a long bus ride, the grounding effect (and energy) of the crystal will help you. Be sure to cleanse it nightly.

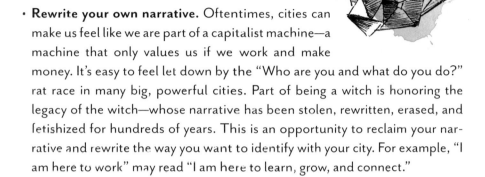

- **Rewrite your own narrative.** Oftentimes, cities can make us feel like we are part of a capitalist machine—a machine that only values us if we work and make money. It's easy to feel let down by the "Who are you and what do you do?" rat race in many big, powerful cities. Part of being a witch is honoring the legacy of the witch—whose narrative has been stolen, rewritten, erased, and fetishized for hundreds of years. This is an opportunity to reclaim your narrative and rewrite the way you want to identify with your city. For example, "I am here to work" may read "I am here to learn, grow, and connect."

- **Do good.** This is our greatest magic. When we do good, we feel good, and we build a world we want to be in. Donate money, goods, or clothing if you can. Protest. Join community action groups that align with your values. Vote. Speak up. Help your community by showing up to it. Check in with friends and neighbors. Volunteer your time at food drives, harm reduction organizations, parks, and shelters. Plant a tree. Get your hands dirty in the local community garden. Plant herbs on your windowsill and give sachets of basil to your neighbors. Offer courses and workshops to help others in your area. Use your platform, big or small, to promote local businesses. Choose your friends with intention and nourish your friendships. Join a coven and learn from them.

- **Make mundane, public spaces sacred.** There are likely hundreds of nooks and crannies sprinkled around your city. Take note of ones that compel you; they can ground you and provide a stopping place for rest on weary days. You may have several—near your home, near your subway entrance, near your

train station, or near your job. Think of statues, museum steps, rose bushes, park benches, one of the massive trees on the edge of a park, elevators that allow you to pause and breathe before stepping out into the world, street art or graffiti, your favorite little cafés, cemetery paths, religious spaces, portals (entrance ways to parks or plazas), and any occult art that you've discovered. Turn to them when you need a breather or a space for reflection or breath work breaks. Leave flowers at your favorite graves, statues, or benches, or leave an offering under the tree before your home or office. Visit these places during walks, on breaks, or on your way home. Make place into ritual.

....

- **Rely on your chosen family.** Many of us move to cities alone, which means we are separated from our family or the community in which we grew up. Chosen family are the ones that support us when times are hard and sad. Get a group chat together for "I'm having a rough day" support. Don't underestimate your coven!

....

- **Carry moon water mist in your bag.** Find a small glass spray bottle and fill it with moon water (with a rose oil if you'd like) to take wherever you go. Make it with each new moon and spritz it on your face when you're out in public dodging crowds and rushing to meetings. The physical sensation will help to ground you.

- **Find a coven to make magic with.** This may help you feel less alone and less frustrated by city life by infusing the life with magic. Many of us city folk are lucky to have occult bookshops or metaphysical shops that hold events (a great place to meet magical folks!). You can also use Meetup or find others via social media. If there is no event space or witch community near you, it may be worth it to see if occult or metaphysical shops in other areas host Zoom or other online events and classes where you can learn, listen, and chat with others.

- **Engage with the art of your city.** Oftentimes, city life feels draining because we are stuck in a rut—home to work and then back to home. Go to a poetry reading, wander in the museum, walk through a neighborhood that inspires you, try a new coffee shop you've heard good things about, join a city tour, find the hidden gems via Atlas Obscura, or visit a beautiful spot tourists love that you tend to ignore. Feel the pulse of the city and listen to its voice (see **chapter 4 for more on connecting with your city's artistry**).

- **Ask the otherworld for help.** Light a candle and ask the city spirits, archetypes, energies, or your higher self to help you find your peace, love, and enjoyment again. Sometimes when we say it aloud—and admit we need help ask for help—we get it. Notice what happens next; often this little ritual opens portals, showing us and throwing us reminders of why we love our space. I've often felt disillusioned in the city, only to be invited to an intimate gathering or to come upon a new resource that changes the way I see things or the way I feel.

- **Acknowledge the shit.** Write a list of the most frustrating aspects of city life, read it aloud with vigor and intent, and then burn it. Flush the remnants down the toilet so the city itself can work its magic. Demand that the frustrations let up or that you become more adaptable to them. Let the fire kindle your deepest energies and put them into the burning of that list.

- **Tell your story and invite others to do the same.** Host a poetry reading night at a pub or in your living room. Share your poetry and stories and artwork of city life; reclaim your narrative. Reflect on the good. Find gratitude. Tell the truth. Mourn what you've lost to the city. In that space, the energy can make way for energetic and personal shifts that help us reframe and recalibrate our place in the city.

- **Create a sigil for peace and adaptability and carry it with you in your bag or in your pocket on rough days.** For an extra boost, create a simple sigil for this purpose that you can create during a walk in the park. By using your body itself to create a sigil, you collaborate with the earth to focus energy on your desired outcome. You may need to draw it out first and use the drawing as a map. Stick to easy movements. (see **Sacred Sigils pp.75**).

....

• **Become anonymous.** Embrace anonymity, dress up, and experience the city as an observer. Say nothing. Be anyone you want to be. Inhabit your own mystery. Find the music in silence. Remember what it's like to observe and not partake. Just experience it (see **Helm of Darkness pp. 114**).

....

• **Get out of blocked spaces.** If you feel you are blocked creatively, physically, or energetically—usually due to lack of light or air flow—find a space that is open and receptive and fluid. This may be on the top of a building or in the middle of a green park.

HYPERCONNECTEDNESS AND THE SACRED: KNOWING WHEN TO TURN OFF

We are all living a hyperconnected life; we can have or know or do anything—at the very least as a student or voyeur or lurker—by using the internet. Our avatars, or digital selves, are, in some ways, always available. We are always being watched and we can always partake in watching. There are definitive perks to this connectivity; these are also the same perks that cities provide—access to information and community, and a sense of being part of something moving, growing, and changing.

And yet the downsides to this constant "on-ness" are real. Many people feel if they live in a city, then they must be doing "city things" or they're somehow wasting their time ("I don't get to the museum enough," my friends and I always gripe). They feel they haven't earned their keep or space in a city if they aren't always connecting, engaging, performing. It's that same need for hyperconnectedness that keeps so many of us on social media—lest we stop being real or "active" or relevant.

Where city magic may sometimes seem to be a magic of doing and going and watching and partaking, it is *also* a magic of tuning into the sacredness of Nothing. Of sitting and being. Of undoing our self-expectations. Of declining the need to prove how much we deserve our space. We don't always have to be available or on the go. We don't have to drink fancy martinis and go to "All the Places." We don't have to work so hard we lose touch with ourselves. We can find the sacred in simply being part of the breathing network all around us, simply by having a heartbeat in its center.

If you are feeling pulled to constantly be on, connected, or active, we can take some gentle action:

• Put your phone away (create a space where you put your phone—like a special box—that feels like a threshold) and open your window. Listen to the sounds. Be alive in the moment.

• Find the things in your city that require no knowledge of "cool spots" or hours of operation. These could be a seaport waterside walk, a public green space, a cemetery, a mural—places where you can be human and alive without having to engage or be "on."

- Make an agenda of joy that doesn't involve having to be available or "on" or engaged or performative in public or on the internet.

- Say no. If you don't want to do that thing all of your friends are doing, if you don't want to go out to that fancy poetry reading or that trivia night at the pub, if you don't want to be online all the time—don't.

- Work through feelings of compulsion to be part of the action by engaging in thoughtful self-asessment: Do you really want to do that thing? Is there something else that makes you feel better?

- Are there lifestyle changes you can make that resonate more with you and feed your spiritual, physical, and psychological needs?

- Find balance. Are there days you can devote to being engaged and active and busy —and days you can assign to rest and click the "off" switch?

- What are three small rituals you can build into your day to ensure your presentness and stillness? Ideas: Pulling a midday tarot card, meditating in silence or in the hum of a crowd, or writing a poem about what you notice around you may be a good start.

- Read *How to Not Always Be Working: A Toolkit for Creativity and Radical Self-Care* by Marlee Grace

- Journal: How do you feel in your heart, mind, and body when you turn the phone or computer off, remove the apps, or let yourself stay home and do nothing? Do you have a fear of missing out? What can fulfill you in a deeper way?

"Arriving at each new city, the traveler finds again a past of his that he did not know he had: the foreignness of what you no longer are or no longer possess lies in wait for you in foreign, unpossessed places."

— ITALO CALVINO

JOURNEY

TAPPING INTO THE MAGIC
OF OTHER CITIES

TRAVELING TO NEW CITIES IS a way of experiencing the hues of the human condition. If the world is a body, then each city is a pulse point, an organ. Each city is a constellation—which sun sign is your city?—with its own shape and narrative, a place that has a unique set of qualities.

We often come away from travel knowing if a city is "my city." Two winters ago, I traipsed through the winter markets and bustling streets of Vienna and Prague, the cold, wide skies a fixture in our experience. In Vienna, I felt almost nothing; my gut didn't "ding," and my heart didn't sing. In Prague, though, I stayed up late talking in cellar bars and stood before the Prague Orloj, its medieval astronomical clock, feeling right at home. My dreams were vivid, nearly prescient. And I was full of inspiration and energy. There are just some cities that speak to you, that align with your own energy, that feel like your own Atlantis—mythic, ideal, superior, eternal.

They don't have to be foreign cities, either. I've felt the incredible energy shifts in the US. In Las Cruces, New Mexico I felt the history of Mexico while walking through Mesilla; and in Salem, Massachusetts, I spoke to the dead.

Unless you return to a site over and over again, it's hard to establish a very deep connection—although you know when the ingredients are there. But every city has many faces (and many masks). In this section, I offer a few last ideas and rituals of connection, curiosity, and magic for the intrepid traveler. Be sure to pack your travel altar (see **The Portable Altar pp. 97**).

Witches, remember: Stay safe energetically (don't be afraid to sprinkle some salt around your doorway, light a protection candle in the dark, or charge an amulet for safety). Stay safe physically. Be aware of weirdos and creeps. Be mindful of how you engage with other cultures, honor the land and its history, and respect the boundaries of closed cultures and traditions. And before you go, I recommend you research the witchy and magical history in the places you travel, for this can tell you a lot about the culture (I especially recommend *Witch Hunt: A Traveler's Guide to the Power and Persecution of the Witch* Kristen J. Sollee as well as others. See **Resources**).

CREATE A TRAVEL ALTAR

Travel is an *immense* privilege. It can be expensive, hard to pull off if you've got a full-time office job, family demands, or a disability.

Many witches have manifested their travels by pouring energy and focus into making them come true, but manifestation only works in alignment with what is possible. Know that while creating a travel altar is a wonderful way of putting that energy out in the universe, *real* limitations and barriers do exist. Race, class, and gender all play into how we experience travel. That is a fact.

If you want to travel or have current travel plans, a travel altar is a great way to help manifest, plan for, or raise energy for a trip. If this is a trip to an ancestral homeland or for some personally meaningful circumstance, even better. The altar will offer a chance for you to spend a few moments each day visualizing the trip and the energies you'd like to get out of it.

It may include:
- A photo of the place you want to go
- A map
- A written list of sites you want to see
- A poem written in or about the city, displayed and written out beautifully
- Notes in the local language or dialect

- Ancestral objects, heirlooms, or gifts
- Perfumes or beauty items from the area (think French perfume or origami earrings)
- Wines, liquors, or foods you associate with the place
- Associated colors
- A love letter to the city
- City mottos (almost every city in the world has one)
- Keys to represent liminality and portals

Where do you want to visit, and what will you place upon your travel altar?

A RITUAL AND INCANTATION FOR SAFE TRAVELS

Before leaving your home, you'll want to prepare a sacred space by lighting a candle and visualizing the energy of successful travel and safety. See yourself going through the motions—boarding the plane or bus, arriving, seeing the sights, and feeling safe.

For this ritual, you'll need:
- A candle
- A piece of paper
- String or yarn

Quiet your mind and come up with an incantation you can memorize for your trip. It often helps to use poetic language or musicality (which feels sacred and chant-like to repeat). Here are a few of my own:

I am safe in the arms of London, where the skies watch over me and the earth cradles my feet.

Italy, Italy. I am safe in Italy. Italy, Italy, surrounded by ancestors and history.

You want your incantation to feel personal, to specify the place or places you are going, and the energy and emotion you'd like to manifest. For example, while in Italy, I chose to call on ancestors (as I am Sicilian); and in London, I called on nature to keep me safe. I've always loved the sky in London and felt an affinity with it from the first time I saw it, so it now figures into my sacred work. You may also choose to call on gods, city deities, archetypes, or spirits out loud and in your incantation—particularly if they are associated with the place you are traveling (just be sure they aren't part of a closed culture!).

Next, write the incantation on a piece of paper, charge the paper with protective energy. Feel the energy radiate generously and lovingly from the earth, up through your feet, up into your hands, and into the words on the paper. Next, roll it into a scroll. Tie it tightly shut with a string. This holds the energy, casts the spell, and should not be untied. Take this scroll with you on your trip and keep it safe. Recite the incantation to yourself as you board transportation, walk through significant thresholds (like border controls or state lines), or when you need a boost.

What is your incantation? What will you conjure in your travels?

DREAMING ABROAD: LOOKING FOR MEANINGFUL MESSAGES IN THE MUNDANE

"We travel, some of us forever, to seek other states, other lives, other souls."

—ANAÏS NIN

Ah, the fever dream that is travel—like you're moving through a blip in time, transient, existing temporarily in another state, another way of being, almost another life. When we travel, we are setting our antennas to "receptor" mode, in a way; we are at our witchiest selves—tuned in, frequencies at the ready, intuition on high alert.

When we travel, we sleep in new places, in new beds, in new rooms facing strange directions. We are surrounded by different energies, different beliefs, and different languages. This beautiful strangeness filters into our subconscious, and often we receive messages from whatever energy is flitting around us—curious about who we are, and perhaps in alignment with our receptive nature. Sometimes, what needs to find us finds us when we travel.

In your travel grimoire, be sure to record your dreams—noting colors, textures, voices, people, faces, spaces, moods, tones, feelings, and substorylines. Sometimes you can see a beautiful house in a dream but you feel a sorrow underneath it all. Sometimes historical figures visit us in dreams when we travel. Sometimes local symbols pop up. What are they telling us? What should we know about where we are staying or sleeping? Is the land you are on colonized? Is it sacred? Ask questions of history and do a bit of research.

Sometimes, we have anxious travel dreams—loss of control, dark alleyways that we weren't meant to stumble down, languages that make no sense. While this is normal, you can ease your anxiety by listening and *taking heed*; double check your bag for your passport, and be sure to cue up your map at night. Your intuition is your friend during travel.

In a village just outside of London, I dreamed of a field of magpies landing before me in a field. It felt serendipitous, holy, good. In New York City, I don't see magpies, so this felt significant to me. I started paying attention to England's magpies whenever I saw them in my waking life, and they filled me with a sense of love and peace and safety.

Solo Travel Meditations: On Sacred Archetypes and Trusting the Experience

On a solo trip to Campania, Italy, I felt *so alone* on so many nights. And I *was* alone, sans car and sans friends or guide—four thousand miles from home up on a mountain in a tiny commune. The same volcano that buried ancient Pompeii loomed in the distance. *There is no way down the mountain now,* I told myself. *There is nothing but your own mind.*

But being alone is not the same as loneliness. And I learned that quickly once I opened up to the energies around me. The people in the market, the people who brought me limoncello, the people who steered our boats from island to island, the people who directed me to the nearest *whatever it is*, the tourists who saw me sitting alone and asked me to dine with them—they were everywhere. Those small slivers of kindness and those quick conversations were a reminder we are alone, *but always connected* to other people, and to the earth, and to the stories around us.

I started to pay attention to the stories and myths of the land—especially when I saw that my blue and gold room was called the *Parthenope Room*. This felt like an initiation, a welcoming. I only remotely knew of this siren, Parthenope, that she was one of the many who lived in the waters of Sorrento. The day that I arrived, I fell into a deep, feverish sleep—as if I were lulled by the siren song.

The next day, on the way to Amalfi and Positano, we passed Li Galli, an archipelago of little islands, where Ulysses's sailors were said to be sought out by the sirens, including Parthenope. Of course, sailors would crash in wild waters against these jutting rocks, only to blame the voice of women for their misfortune.

As I traveled by water the next few weeks, I realized Parthenope taught me something—that even in beauty there are dark moments. Songs and deaths go hand in hand. But it is up to me find the light. I can find it on islands, and I can find it in myself.

Traveling alone can be painful—especially for weeks at a time or when we feel disconnected from everyone we know. In these moments, look for the light. Remember the earth sees you and is here with you. It reminds you we *can* and *do* survive, like ancient stories and myths, and that being alone gives us resilience.

Take note of what is around you when you travel: street names, room names, boat names, strangers' names. *What is the energy of the place, and how does it make you feel? What is the city known for? How does its people, food, wine, and nature make you feel?* Note the moon phase. Note the local mythology. Note the place's history of witchcraft and folklore. Note the colors. Note the nature. *What speaks to you? What makes you feel less alone? What comforts you? What can you take with you and hold inside your heart on your solo journey? And how has being alone to experience it all made it sharper and more meaningful?*

There are messages of support and alignment everywhere if you pay attention. *What is the message? What have you learned on your solo travels? What do you hope to learn on a solo travel?* It doesn't need to be far to be meaningful.

In the end, city magic is entirely your own, home-grown and hand-sewn by your city, your own belief systems, and your own vision. Poetry is born between you and your city. How you relate to a space — be it your own or somewhere far away — is a unique energy exchange. Nourish that. Keep your eyes open, your heart curious, and your rituals intentional. Ask the walls of your bedroom to hold you. Notice how the architecture changes your mood. Create an altar for your home spirit. Offer a stranger a helping hand on the subway stairs. Watch how summer ushers in a new divinity. Write poems for a strange, new city. Feel the energy shift between a green space and an intersection. And let the city's constant movement remind you that while life is ever-changing, the relationships and rituals we tend to in our spaces give us deep meaning.

RESOURCES

Below are recommendations that serve a few purposes: to encourage you to dive even deeper into ideas I present within this book, to enrich the conversation around city magic and magical traveling, and to serve as catalysts for creativity in your own city experience.

The Magical Writing Grimoire: Use the Word as Your Wand for Magic, Manifestation & Ritual, Lisa Marie Basile
Light Magic for Dark Times: More than 100 Spells, Rituals, and Practices for Coping in a Crisis, Lisa Marie Basile
Witch Hunt: A Traveler's Guide to the Power and Persecution of the Witch, Kristen J. Sollee
Treadwell's Book of Plant Magic, Christina Oakley Harrington
Urban Magick: A Guide for the City Witch, Diana Rajchel
Green Witchcraft: A Practical Guide to Discovering the Magic of Plants, Herbs, Crystals, and Beyond, Paige Vanderbeck
Witchery: Embrace the Witch Within, Juliet Diaz
Italian Folk Magic: Rue's Kitchen Witchery, Mary-Grace Fahrun
The Tradition of Household Spirits: Ancestral Lore and Practices, Claude Lecouteux
Astrology for Real Life: A Workbook for Beginners (A No B.S. Guide for the Astro-Curious), Theresa Reed
Practical Sigil Magic: Creating Personal Symbols for Success, Frater U.:D.:
Queering Your Craft: Witchcraft from the Margins, Cassandra Snow
Queer Magic: LGBT+ Spirituality and Culture from around the World, Tomás Prower
Intuitive Witchcraft: How to Use Intuition to Elevate Your Craft, Astrea Taylor
Demons and Spirits of the Land: Ancestral Lore and Practices, Claude Lecouteux
Weave the Liminal: Living Modern Traditional Witchcraft, Laura Tempest Zakroff

Enchantments: A Modern Witch's Guide to Self-Possession, Mya Spalter

Revolutionary Witchcraft: A Guide to Magical Activism, Sarah Lyons

You Were Born for This: Astrology for Radical Self-Acceptance, Chani Nicholas

HausMagick: Transform Your Home with Witchcraft, Erica Feldmann

The Complete Book of Moon Spells: Rituals, Practices, and Potions for Abundance, Michael Herkes

City Magick: Spells, Rituals, and Symbols for the Urban Witch, Christopher Penczak

How to Not Always Be Working: A Toolkit for Creativity and Radical Self-Care, Marlee Grace

Women Who Run with the Wolves: Myths and Stories of the Wild Woman Archetype, Clarissa Pinkola Estés

The Wander Society, Keri Smith

Braiding Sweetgrass: Indigenous Wisdom, Scientific Knowledge, and the Teachings of Plants, Robin Wall Kimmerer

The Poetics of Space, Gaston Bachelard

Poet in New York, Federico García Lorca

Wanderlust: A History of Walking, Rebecca Solnit

Taking the Waters: Spirit, Art, Sensuality, Alev Lytle Croutier

Earth Grids: The Secret Patterns of Gaia's Sacred Sites, Hugh Newman

The Flowers of Evil, Charles Baudelaire

Follow me at https://www.instagram.com/ritual_poetica and https://www.instagram.com/lisamariebasile for city rituals and writing prompts. More resources and links to city poetry can be found at my website, https://www.lisamariebasile.com.

ACKNOWLEDGMENTS

A massive thank you to my editor, Meredith, and my supporters, readers, Luna Luna family, and to everyone who has read and shared my books.

Thank you to my family for raising me to be the magical person I am, especially Mom. Thank you to AT who encouraged me to write this book when I doubted myself, and to all my peers and friends who shared their ideas. And then there is my Benjamin who always shows up to me with love and enthusiasm, and to the constant conversations around *City Witchery*.

But most of all, I want to thank the many city witches, activists, artists, creators, writers, and poets who make our cities better, more magical, and more compassionate places—especially during 2020, when everything changed. I see you.

ABOUT

LISA MARIE BASILE (she/her) is a poet, word witch, essayist, editor, and chronic illness awareness advocate living in New York City. She's the founder and creative director of *Luna Luna Magazine,* and the creator of ritual poetica, a curiosity project dedicated to exploring the intersection of writing, creativity, healing, and sacredness.

She regularly creates dialogue and writes about intentionality and ritual, accessibility, creativity, poetry, foster care, mental health, family trauma, healing, and chronic illness. She is also the author of *The Magical Writing Grimoire, Light Magic for Dark Times*, and a few poetry collections.

Her essays and other work can be found in the *New York Times, Narratively, Sabat Magazine, Witch Craft Magazine, Refinery 29, Self, Healthline, Entropy, On Loan From the Cosmos, Catapult, BUST, Bustle*, and more. She earned a master's degree in writing from The New School and studied literature and psychology as an undergraduate at Pace University.